WHAT'S TO BECOME OF THE LEGAL PROFESSION?

Michael H. Trotter

ISBN-13: 9781534903692
ISBN-10: 1534903690
Library of Congress Control Number: 2016920855
CreateSpace Independent Publishing Platform
North Charleston, South Carolina

I dedicate this book to my children An and Bill with great appreciation for their love, friendship and support

CONTENTS

PREFACE

My legal career began in the summer of 1960 (after my first year of law school) as a *summer boarder* in the 15 lawyer Atlanta firm of Alston, Sibley, Miller, Spann & Shackelford (now Alston & Bird). Over the ensuing 55 years I have been a partner in the Alston firm, a senior partner in two entrepreneurial law firms, a partner in the Kilpatrick law firm, and a partner in the new model law firm of Taylor English Duma LLP where I am now a senior counsel.

It has been my good fortune to have experienced first-hand the legal profession's evolution since 1960 as reflected on the following pages. I continue to confront in my practice every day the challenges faced by practicing lawyers, law firms and law departments. As a result my perspective is different from many of the consultants and academics responsible for most of the current dire predictions about the future of the profession.

Almost from the beginning it was my privilege to work on significant projects with many of the leading law firms in the United States. I learned a great deal about the practice of law and law firm operations during these engagements and from the friendships they engendered.

In the early 1990s I taught courses at the Emory University Law School that may have been the first, and certainly were among the first, law school courses on law firm economics and operations. I have written two books, *Profit and the Practice of Law* (1997, reissued 2012) and *Declining Prospects* (2012) as well as numerous articles about the economics and operations of law firms in the United States from the end of World War II to the current day.

Pig in a Poke, the Uncertain Advantages of Large and Highly Leveraged Law Firms in America is the chapter I wrote for the ABA's published book *Raise the Bar — Real World Solutions for a Troubled Profession* (2007). And in recent years I served as an expert witness on law firm economics and operations in the Heller Ehrman bankruptcy and as a legal advisor in connection with the Howrey bankruptcy.

In October of 2013, I had the honor of serving as the Keynote Presenter at the NALP Foundation's National Forum on *The Future of the Legal Profession*. Many of the participants including law school deans, major firm managing partners, corporate general counsel, law firm consultants and recruiters shared their own thoughts on the subject. Since then I have had other opportunities to further elaborate on the future of the legal profession and to learn more about it every day.

I served as Chairman of the Law Firm Finance Committee of the Law Practice Division of the American Bar Association in the 2015-2016 year and continue as a member of the committee, and I am currently teaching courses at the Emory University School of

Law about the evolution of the legal profession and law practice economics, and about the future of the legal profession.

Concerns about the future of the profession are evidenced by a constant flow of new books and articles on the topic in the legal press. *What's to Become of the Legal Profession?* has been written to carefully analyze our prospects as a profession and in part to ease these concerns. Others will continue to have much to say on the subject. I hope that we will be able to dispel the ubiquitous pessimism about the future of the practice of law in the United States and in the process find the desire and capability to further improve the quality and availability of legal services for our clients and potential clients.

I am indebted to my colleagues and friends John Hopkins and John Gross for reviewing drafts of this book and for their insights and suggestions that have greatly improved it. I am equally indebted to my daughter An Trotter, former Senior Director of Administration for the Law Department of Viacom, Inc. and now the Senior Director of Legal & Compliance Operations of the HARMAN International Law Department, for her many suggestions and insights with respect to the operations of law departments and law firms. I am also indebted to my son Bill Trotter, a reporter for the *Bangor Daily News*, for his assistance in reviewing and editing this book. It has also benefited from the able work of Irene Talerico, who has worked with me as an editorial assistant.

INTRODUCTION

This book is about the future of the legal profession in the United States. We have heard from some legal consultants and academics that "serious, irreversible change is about to shake the legal market to its core" (Jordan Furlong in *Evolutionary Road—A Strategic Guide to your Law Firm's Future*) and that "Legal institutions and lawyers are at a crossroads…and are poised to change more radically over the next two decades than they have over the last two centuries" (Richard Susskind in his 2013 book, *Tomorrow's Lawyers: An Introduction to Your Future*). Susskind has also said that "the legal profession in the future will bear little resemblance to the way in which lawyers have worked in the past. The 21st century lawyer will, I believe, take on a whole different set of rules from the 20th Century lawyer."

I do not agree with these disturbing predictions and many similar ones about the future of the legal profession, nor do I think that the challenges we now face as a profession are any more intimidating than the ones we have already experienced and survived since the end of World War II. There will continue to be significant changes in what has become the legal industry, but the legal profession has developed the maturity and self-assurance necessary to deal with whatever the future holds.

The transformation that has already occurred since the end of World War II has been extraordinary—so many things about the way law is practiced have changed! Nonetheless in this process the legal profession has demonstrated an exceptional capacity to adjust to the changing environment in which we practice our trade.

CHAPTER ONE

The Evolution of the Legal Profession

The following significant changes have occurred in the legal profession in the United States since 1945:

(1) *At the end of World War II* in the United States and most other countries there were relatively few laws, regulations and regulatory agencies, and there were even fewer international agencies and organizations. Few businesses in the United States were engaged in international commerce.

Today in the United States we have the same governments (federal and state), but most are much larger, have many more departments and regulatory agencies, and have greatly expanded responsibilities. We also have many more local governments and agencies of government. Most other countries also have in place a larger and growing body of laws, governmental departments and agencies. Many foreign based businesses are actively engaged in commerce in the United States, and many businesses based in the

United States are also engaged in international commerce. There are also many international agreements, organizations and agencies that seek to manage commercial and political relationships among the nations of the world.

(2) *In 1950* there were 221,600 lawyers in the United States; one for every 687 Americans.

Today there are 1,315,500 lawyers in the United States; one for every 246 Americans.

(3) *In 1953* there were 13,111 first year law students enrolled in U.S. law schools.

In 2015 there were 37,058 first year students enrolled in U.S. law schools (down from 52,488 in 2010).

(4) *In 1961* tuition at Harvard Law School was $1,250 a year that, adjusted for inflation, would be about $10,000 today.

Now many private law schools (including Harvard) are five times or more expensive charging annual tuition in a range of $50,000 to $65,000 a year. Other related expenses can increase costs by an additional $25,000 to $30,000 a year. Tuition at state law schools has also increased significantly and generally by a higher percentage than the tuition increases at most private law schools. Many law school students are incurring debt of $150,000 or more to pay for their law school educations, and many also have additional debt incurred to finance their undergraduate educations.

(5) *In 1960* most law firms had one office in one city and were tiny by today's standards. The largest firm based in the United States in 1960 had 125 lawyers and the largest firm in Atlanta had 21.

In 2015 the firm with the most lawyers in the United States was Morgan Lewis with 1,747. The United States based Baker & McKenzie had an international headcount of 4,363 lawyers and 78 offices in 47 countries. There were 22 law firms operating in the United States that had more than 1,000 lawyers each and an additional 60 firms with more than 500 lawyers. Many of these firms had offices in multiple American cities and several foreign ones. Dentons, the largest firm headquartered outside the USA, has more than 7,000 lawyers as a result of recent mergers.

(6) *In the 1950s* most lawyers were not well paid; a 1964 article in *Law Office Economics and Management* published by the American Bar Association lamented that during the 1950s the legal profession was rapidly becoming "an impoverished profession." The starting annual salary for new associates at the major New York City firms in 1962 was $7,500, the equivalent of about $59,000 today, and in Atlanta it was $6,000 (up from $3,600 in 1960), the equivalent of about $47,000 today. The highest paid senior partner in Atlanta in 1962 was rumored to have earned about $85,000 a year including trustee's, executor's and director's fees which would be the equivalent of about $688,000 today.

In 2015 major firm lawyers at every level were much better paid than they were in 1962. Starting salaries for associates at such firms ranged from $135,000 to $160,000 a year or more (in mid-2016 a number of firms increased their starting pay to $180,000). Ninety of the Am Law 200 firms reported average annual compensation for equity partners ("Profits Per Partner" or "PPP") in excess of $1 million, the PPP of the most prosperous firm was $6,600,000 and PPP at Atlanta's most prosperous major firm was over $2,300,000.

(7) *In the 1950s* partners were personally responsible for debts and obligations of their firms; malpractice insurance was a new innovation, and law firms had not started using limited liability partnerships and companies.

Today partners are not legally responsible for the debts and obligations of their law firms, most of which are organized as limited liability entities, unless their personal actions give rise to such obligations or they have personally guaranteed obligations of their firms. Moreover most firms carry substantial liability insurance protecting their lawyers from claims arising out of their professional practice (in addition to customary forms of business insurance). The resulting insulation from individual liability has had a profound effect on the size, organization and operations of law firms.

(8) *Prior to the* **mid-*1970*s** it was a violation of the cannons of legal ethics for a lawyer or firm to advertise. It was also a violation to solicit the legal work of a business or individual. Consequently, most of the established firms were at little risk of losing their clients to another lawyer or firm.

Today the pursuit of clients is largely without restriction, and every firm has to work every day to retain the clients they have and to pursue others in order to enlarge their practice and to replace those they lose or whose work diminishes.

(9) *In 1950* the services most firms provided were paid for through retainers or fixed standard fees for the types of services rendered. Many bar associations had "Minimum Fee Schedules" that covered routine matters.

Today a great deal of legal work is paid for by the hour at rates that have increased substantially in excess of inflation over the past 50 plus years, while alternative types of fee arrangements (including a return to retainers and fixed fee arrangements) are becoming more common.

(10) *In the 1950s* many major law firms did not maintain time records, and partners were usually compensated based on their seniority rather than on the hours they charged to clients, the fees they generated, or the clients they serviced. Firm clients were generally considered to be assets of the firm rather than of particular partners.

Today all law firms maintain records of the hours spent by their individual lawyers on their various projects, and client control and fees collected from such clients have become the key determiners of partner compensation at most firms. Many clients identify more closely with the partner responsible for their work than with the partner's law firm.

(11) *In the 1950s* most lawyers practiced by themselves or in small firms of a few lawyers. The larger firms usually had two categories of lawyers (partners and associates), and in many of these firms partners substantially outnumbered associates.

Now in many large firms equity partners constitute 20% or less of billable personnel, with the remaining 80% consisting of various categories of billable-employees including nonequity partners, counsel, associates, career associates, contract lawyers, leased lawyers, legal assistants and other types of unlicensed billable employees.

(12) *In the 1950s* because there were relatively few associates and no billable nonlawyer employees, the partners' incomes came primarily from their own work rather than from the work of their employees.

Today equity partners provide a much smaller percentage of the legal services provided by most major firms. As a result most equity partners receive a substantial percentage of their income from profits generated by the work of their employees.

(13) *In the 1950s* the work of a firm's nonlawyer employees was viewed as a part of the firm's overhead and not charged to clients.

Today most law firms charge for the work of many of their nonlawyer personnel on an hourly rate basis.

(14) *In the 1950s* although lawyers were, as they are now, free agents, they rarely exercised their freedom to move to other firms, and it was generally considered inappropriate to recruit lawyers from competitors.

Today the "lateral hiring" of lawyers has become the leading growth strategy of most major law firms.

(15) *In the 1950s* most partners were generalists rather than specialists (many firms did not have departmentalized areas of practice).

Today most large law firms have numerous departments, virtually every partner is a specialist, and most associates are specialists in training.

(16) *In the 1950s* most of the knowledge and experience that firms had to sell was in the heads of their partners or in client matter files rather than in knowledge management systems. Generally, available legal knowledge was found in court reports, legal encyclopedias, case books, treatises and a few specialized loose-leaf services.

Today most large law firms and law departments have computer based proprietary legal knowledge and know-how management systems supplemented by commercially available knowledge and experience programs on the Internet or in print in the form of articles, checklists, practice notes, related cases, and standard documents and clauses relevant to legal matters and issues of all kinds. Clients and their law departments can access much of this knowledge easily and quickly without paying a law firm to find it.

(17) *In 1950* very few businesses or organizations had an in-house general counsel—much less a law department.

In 2014 virtually every business or organization of any significant size has an in-house general counsel *and* its own law department, with two large U.S. companies having more than 1,000 in-house attorneys, and dozens of others having hundreds.

(18) *In the 1950s* few firms had a formal managing partner or a management committee. Decisions were made by consensus among the partners, with some partners having more influence than others.

Today most medium-sized to large firms have full-time lawyer executives as well as senior nonlawyer or nonpracticing lawyer executives managing their operations, and most have partners' committees, boards of directors, or executive committees approving firm policies and overseeing firm operations.

(19) *In the 1950s* associates learned how to practice law from the partners in the firms with whom they worked.

Currently the high leverage of most large firms and compensation considerations make it difficult, if not impossible, for the equity partners to train their lawyer and nonlawyer billable employees— as a result that task falls to junior partners, senior associates, and continuing legal education courses. Some law firms employ trainers to oversee their training programs and to coach their younger lawyers, and most sizable firms conduct in-house continuing legal education programs. Increasingly law firms are pressuring law schools to provide the training that the firms formerly provided themselves.

(20) *In the 1950s* there were very, very few women working as lawyers.

Today almost half of all law school students are women, approximately 36% of all lawyers are women, and women occupy prominent positions of leadership in many law firms, law departments, legal associations and the judiciary.

(21) *Following World War II* partners would often serve on boards of directors of the clients they represented, and some served as executive officers of clients as well.

Today it is rare for private practice lawyers to serve on the boards of directors of publically owned businesses, and even rarer to serve as an officer or on the board of a publicly held client represented by their firm.

(22) *In 1960* technology consisted of a dictating machine, a typewriter, carbon paper, Correcto-Type, a Thermofax machine, and a dial telephone.

Large law firms *today* spend millions of dollars on their computer, printing and communications systems as well as on hardware and software to support every aspect of their operations including record keeping, client recruitment and retention, personnel recruitment, management, project management, legal research and knowledge management, document production, communications, and financial management.

(23) *In the 1950s and early 1960s* the Georgia Bar admitted everyone who had completed two years of law school and passed the state bar exam even though they did not have a law degree and may not have attended an ABA accredited law school. Lawyers were not subject to any continuing legal education requirements.

In most states *today* only graduates with three years of legal education at an ABA accredited law school who have passed the requisite bar exam are permitted to practice law. In order to maintain their licenses to practice lawyers must take continuing legal education courses to maintain and update their legal knowledge and skills.

(24) *For decades* virtually all law school graduates found jobs as lawyers.

In 2015 66.6% of the students graduating from law schools had found work requiring a law degree within ten months of their graduation. An additional 14.5% had found jobs where a JD degree provided an advantage, but was not a requirement.

These many changes and others not listed provide ample evidence of the toughness, creativity and resilience of the legal profession in the United States over the last 70+ years. Most Am Law 200 firms reached their current positions of distinction not by developing and implementing carefully thought-out long-range plans and strategies, but rather by evolving in response to a growing need for legal services and reacting incrementally to changes in the dynamics and economics of the practice of law in the USA and the world over more than seven decades.

CHAPTER TWO

The Key Developments in the Practice of Law since the End of World War II

A mong the many changes identified in Chapter One that have occurred in the operations of the legal profession in the United States (and much of the rest of the world) since the end of World War II, seven have been essential to the creation of the modern major business practice law firm.

The changes are:

(1) The continuing growth and interaction of the economies of the United States and other countries, and of their governments, laws and regulations.

(2) A significant reduction of the financial risks of practicing law in large groups.

(3) The virtual elimination of restraints on the marketing of legal services.

(4) The acceptability of the lateral movement of lawyers from one law firm to another.

(5) The pricing of legal services based on hours worked at fixed rates.

(6) The greatly increased leverage resulting from the expanded use of lawyer employees, and the greatly expanded use of billable nonlawyer personnel to support the delivery of legal services.

(7) Advances in technology that have enabled many of the changes that have occurred.

Without the key changes identified above and discussed below, the major law firms of the 1950s and firms created since could not have grown into the legal service powerhouses they are today.

(1) GROWTH IN ECONOMIES, LAWS AND REGULATIONS

Following World War II there was a tremendous growth in the economies of the United States and the world. At the same time there was a significant growth in the body of law and in the number and size of the administrative and regulatory apparatus of governments—local, state and federal—in the United States and in many other countries. The growing interdependence of the economies of the United States and of other countries created a tremendous growth in the need for more, and more complex, legal relationships and services on both a national and international scale. As a result, there has been a continuing surge of growth in the number of laws, regulations, pronouncements and rulings from governments, courts and administrators that govern most aspects of human activity and enterprise.

(2) Reduction in the Financial Risks of Practicing in Large Groups

The major firms of the past were small, in part because of personal financial liability concerns that discouraged growth in size and geographical expansion. Almost all law firms were organized as general partnerships and therefore each partner was financially at risk for the misconduct or carelessness of every lawyer and every employee in their firm. No one wanted to be in a general partnership with partners they did not know well and trust implicitly to oversee the firm's work and its employees.

Travel was slow, expensive and time consuming, and the only alternatives to personal meetings were the US Mail and long-distance telephone calls. Firms could not monitor the work-product of distant colleagues electronically or participate in video-conferences as they do today. Because of limited and costly travel and communications capability the supervision of hundreds, much less thousands, of lawyers scattered about the country and the world would have been virtually impossible to imagine and manage, and much too risky.

Improved communications including the Internet, and improved transportation alternatives made it much easier and more convenient to operate law firms and law departments with multiple offices. And the creation of professional malpractice insurance for lawyers and law firms in the mid-1940s, and its adoption by most firms over the ensuing 15 years, reduced the risk to partners of a catastrophic personal financial loss resulting from the practice of law. The development of limited liability partnerships in the late 1980s and early 1990s further shielded partners from financial losses caused by the malpractice or misconduct of one of their colleagues or staff. As a result of these developments the financial risks associated with being a partner in a large and geographically dispersed law firm were greatly reduced.

Because profits retained by firms in their capital accounts remained subject to risk, these changes have also encouraged many firms to distribute their profits as soon as possible, decreasing their financial strength.

(3) THE VIRTUAL ELIMINATION OF RESTRAINTS ON THE MARKETING OF LEGAL SERVICES

In the 1950s and 1960s most competition for legal services was local. Major businesses in some states would engage lawyers outside the state on some significant matters, but businesses usually engaged lawyers in the community or state in which their principal executives resided. There was no such thing as a "national law firm" although some of the major eastern firms had a national practice. For the most part lawyers did not have to worry about their clients or potential clients being rushed by firms located in other states or regions.

For many years the solicitation of clients was governed by Cannon 2 of the ABA's Code of Professional Responsibility—mimicked to a substantial degree in the rules of every state bar association—which restricted direct competition for clients among lawyers and law firms. The essential restraint imposed by the Cannon was that a lawyer or law firm could not solicit potential clients directly or through advertising. The penalty for doing so could be disbarment from the practice of law, or at least ostracism by the local bar.

These restrictions on the marketing and soliciting of legal work were overturned by the United States Supreme Court in a series of cases decided in the latter part of the 1970s. As a result, every firm was permitted to compete with every other firm for their clients' business and it became acceptable for law firms to market their services to businesses and individuals represented by their competitors. It also became necessary for law firms to protect their existing client relationships by increasing the cultivation of their own clientele. Lateral hiring became more feasible because firms could solicit the representation of their new colleague's former clients.

This significant change also enabled firms to open offices in new cities with some hope of luring clients away from the established local firms. Major barriers to lateral lawyer movement and geographical expansion had been eliminated.

(4) THE ACCEPTABILITY OF LATERAL MOVEMENT OF LAWYERS BETWEEN LAW FIRMS

After World War II there was no legal or ethical prohibition of lateral lawyer movement between law firms, but there was a deeply engrained taboo within the profession against such moves.

Agency law prohibited then, and prohibits now, a lawyer planning to make a lateral move from soliciting the representation of clients of his existing firm *before* he has given his firm notice of his withdrawal. *After* he left his former firm, Cannon 2 prohibited the relocated lawyer and his new firm from soliciting the legal work of clients represented by his former law firm (as well as clients represented by any other law firm). Consequently, the combination of agency law and Cannon 2 greatly complicated the process of acquiring or moving clients in connection with the lateral movement of lawyers from one firm to another. When Cannon 2 was quashed by the Supreme Court, one of the major impediments to lateral movement between law firms was removed.

The combined effect of the reduction in partner liability exposure, the lifting of the ban on solicitation of other firms' clients, and the erosion of the taboo against lateral lawyer hiring made the creation of many new law firms possible, and greatly facilitated the creation of national law firms.

Several major firms based in the old industrial centers in the Midwest realized that as long as they had a single office in an industrial center with a shrinking economy and clients, their prospects would decline. In the 1980s, several of the nation's most highly regarded firms were based in such an industrial center—Cleveland, Ohio. They included Arter & Hadden, Baker & Hostettler, Jones Day Reavis & Pogue, Squire Sanders & Dempsey, and Thompson Hine & Flory. Each adopted a survival strategy based on geographical expansion by combining with smaller established firms in other major cities located in regions with growing economies, or opening offices with lateral lawyers brought in from firms in those cities, or transferring existing lawyers to the new locations. Many major firms also opened offices in the District of Columbia because of the growing role of the Federal government in American law and business. Other firms, capitalizing on a particular client or personal relationship, opened offices in new locations. The race for national and international dominance had begun.

The success of some of these expansions created a model that has been followed often by major firms seeking to utilize their established name recognition and reputations to grow their practices. In due course, the larger size and geographic diversification came to be seen by many firms as a competitive advantage which led to more major firms developing a presence in large regional cities. At the same time new technologies made it easier and less expensive to manage national or international practices with multiple offices.

Established regional firms began opening new offices as a necessary response to the actions of competitors from other regions that were invading their territory. The major firms began to compete for each other's clients and those of other firms. I note however that the Elite Firms (discussed at length in Chapter 3) have tended to open fewer offices, and have generally not focused their attention on locally situated legal work in regional markets.

During the 1960s and 1970s, as business grew and promising new clients came to the established firms for assistance, older partners continued to view the new clients through their historical perspective as *firm clients* like their other clients of long standing. However, younger partners were often doing most of the work for these new clients, and such clients as well as the lawyers working for them were more likely to see their relationship as personal rather than institutional.

The growth in clientele had also given rise to a growing number of conflicts of interest that prevented firms from representing all of their new prospects, and these conflicts caused many a lateral move, and the creation of many new law firms.

In this same time frame, as hourly billing became the dominant method of charging for legal services and revenue was closely correlated with hours billed, those partners recording the most hours began to feel short-changed by those who were billing less time, but earning as much or more because of their seniority in their firms.

In many firms one or another of these factors led to some partners leaving to form new firms or to cut better deals at other firms. These factors have also often led to adjustments in the allocation of profits among firm partners. Control of a client's legal business became an increasingly important issue with respect to partner status and income.

(5) HOURLY BILLING

Prior to the 1960s many law firms had retainer arrangements with their regular clients that provided for an agreed upon annual payment for all services to be rendered. Services not covered by a retainer were often based on fee schedules maintained by local or state bar associations. In some other matters, time and hourly rates were a part of a multi-factor process for determining a mutually agreeable appropriate fee, but it was unusual for hours and hourly rates alone to determine fees.

In the mid to late 1960s many national clients with law departments started insisting that their outside law firms bill by the hour at mutually agreed fixed hourly rates. At the Alston Firm, Chrysler was the first. The firms were generally skeptical of hourly billing and were uncomfortable with the concept. They thought that the value of their service to their client should be a consideration in determining an appropriate bill. They asked: "Shouldn't we be paid more if we get a great result or if we have to work nights, holidays and weekends to meet your needs?" The clients' response was that they were hiring the best lawyers in the market and expected good results and hard work—all of which had been taken into account in setting the hourly rates.

In due course, law firms discovered the advantages of hourly billing, and the billable hour became the predominant billing relationship between lawyers and their clients.

During the late 1960s and the early 1970s, as hourly billing spread throughout the profession, the rapid growth of the economy and the effects of the Viet Nam War left most of the major firms short of lawyers with more legal work to do than they could comfortably produce. Therefore they did not have the ability or the incentive to overwork projects.

Associates were paid a fixed annual salary and generally moved up in lockstep based on their years of service, and most of the partners were compensated based on their seniority rather than their hours worked. Consequently there was not a direct relationship between the hours worked or billed by lawyers and their compensation. As a result, most did not aggressively bill their time or overwork the matters to which they were assigned. Under these circumstances, the billable hour system worked well for clients and lawyers alike.

Eventually the keeping of time records changed their tenor from one of several billing aids to a measure of the value of the work performed, and the question of the value of the service became confused with the time a lawyer took to provide it. Many lawyers and firms began to think of their role in providing legal services as selling time. As this transformation occurred, considerations of quality, efficiency and results became significantly less important.

This development should not have come as a surprise to corporate counsel because they were the folks who initially had insisted on eliminating considerations of quality, efficiency and results in determining the amount of legal fees they would pay.

In the fullness of time, it was the clients' turn to become skeptical of hourly billing. Dollars collected for client work became a major criterion for determining partner compensation at many firms, and associates were often paid bonuses based on the number of hours they had billed. As a result, in most firms today both partners and associates have a financial incentive to report as many billable hours as they can.

Due to the frailties of human nature some lawyers are tempted to inflate their hours and to overwork projects in order to increase their compensation. Under these circumstances clients are justified in turning a skeptical eye to the bills they receive that are based on hours recorded.

At many firms the hourly billing rate assigned to new associates may be thirty to forty percent of the hourly rate for the most experienced partners. This practice overprices associates' work and underprices the contribution of seasoned lawyers. Today a number of corporate law departments will not pay anything for the work of first or second year associates.

Is every hour of a particular lawyer worth the same amount in dollars regardless of the work being done? Do expert lawyers charge a lower rate for their time if working on an issue about which they are not experts? Should clients be charged for the person doing the work rather than for the work done? These questions are among those that are appropriately raised about the hourly billing system.

There are several alternative ways to price legal work in use today; the contingent fee is one of the oldest and most resilient of these alternatives, but even the contingent fee relationship can be manipulated by lawyers to their advantage. There has been a return to fixed fees agreed upon in advance for some matters that are relatively routine, for multiple matters of similar types, or when there is a reasonable basis for estimating the time and personnel necessary to complete the anticipated work.

There have been some efforts to revive the retainer system. The most notable effort was the Pfizer Legal Alliance experiment. Pfizer's law department identified a group of firms to which it would allocate virtually all of its outside work. At the beginning of the fiscal year the law department allocated most of the law department's annual budget for outside assistance to selected firms in specific dollar amounts to handle all of Pfizer's work in the category assigned to them. The remainder of the budget was then distributed at the end of the year to adjust for unexpected larger work-loads and particularly outstanding work.

It appears that the Alliance concept did not generate a satisfactory outcome for Pfizer and its law firms, and after a few years has been largely abandoned.

There are other alternatives. Some larger companies have identified bundles of work that they put out for competitive bidding to prequalified bidders. In some cases the auction is conducted online for a limited period of time in a way that permits each bidder to see the bids of the other participating firms. Often, but not always, the ultimate low bidder gets the work. I've been told of one such situation where the firm or firms with the highest bids were disqualified from participating in future work for the client.

In the United States we have now had more than 50 years of experience with the hourly billing system. Most lawyers, inside and out, are accustomed to how it works or doesn't work. It remains the predominate method of billing. Properly used, it will continue to play an important role in pricing legal services in the years ahead.

This really isn't surprising given the fact that the compensation of many people across a wide spectrum of jobs in industries and businesses is based on an hourly rate for a set number of hours a day without regard for how hard they work and what they accomplish on any particular day.

(6) GREATLY INCREASED LEVERAGE

Greatly increased leverage (along with higher hourly rates) has been the most significant contributor to increasing equity partner compensation over the last 20 years.

The Depression and World War II adversely affected the size and profitability of the major law firms; following the war most of the major firms consisted primarily of several equity partners supported by a few associates. As the need for legal services began to increase rapidly in the late 1950s and the early 1960s the only way most firms could service the growing demand was to employ more associates and to train them as rapidly as possible. As a result associate leverage increased, and with it partner compensation.

As increased leverage resulted in increased partner compensation no one wanted to earn less, and some realized that further leverage could lead to even higher compensation. In the 1960s and early 1970s, most associates expected to advance to partnership and to participate in the growing profitability. As profits per partner increased, it was not surprising that the legal profession began to attract more young people with a significant interest in earning a lot of money.

At some point for most of the established firms the naturally occurring growth in size, leverage and profitability took on a life of its own. The relatively high markup on associate time compared to partner time encouraged this trend. Growth began to occur for profit's sake; the desire for increased equity partner profits began to drive the need for increased size and increased leverage.

A few of the major eastern firms had long enjoyed the economic benefits of relatively high associate leverage coupled with restricted associate promotion to partnership. In the 1970s the partners in many other major firms realized that they could increase their compensation if they did not continue to promote as many of their associates as they had historically. As a result the percentage of associates who ultimately made partner began to decline.

By the mid-1980s many firms wanted to find a way to keep a higher percentage of their most accomplished associates without advancing them as quickly to partnership and to retain some senior lawyers without making them equity partners. In order to do so they created a new category of *nonequity partner* and expanded their use of the *counsel* category.

They also realized that some of their work could be done by less expensive lawyers who would not qualify to become any sort of partner or counsel or even a standard associate. As a result *career associates, contract lawyers,* and *leased lawyers* became a part of the personnel profile of many firms.

In addition, starting in the 1970s, many firms began to expand their reliance on support personnel who were not lawyers but whose services could nonetheless be billed to clients as legal assistants, paralegals, and consultants.

(a) Nonequity Partners and Counsel—Career Associates and Contract Lawyers

Many firms created a *nonequity* partnership category for the senior associates they wished to retain without full promotion to equity partner status that would have diluted equity partner compensation. This category and the counsel category were also used for *service partners*—competent and experienced technicians without significant books of business. Firms creating a nonequity partner position typically rationalized that they were doing so as a necessary way station for senior associates to test their suitability for equity partnership and to provide additional preparation for higher levels of responsibility. Nonequity partners were generally identified to the public only as partners.

The little used category of counsel came into greater use as a designation for some of the senior lawyers moving from other law firms, or for some expert lawyers who were basically service lawyers who did not control substantial amounts of business.

The terms partner and counsel were widely recognized by clients and other lawyers as titles attesting to the experience, maturity and competence of the lawyers so classified and, as a result, clients were willing to pay more for the services of a partner or a counsel than for the services of an associate, and clients felt more comfortable if their important work was being done by, or at least supervised by, a partner or counsel. Mid-level lawyers wanted the title of partner even if they were not participating as equity partners because the title signified that they had a higher level of professional competence than an associate.

In due course, nonequity partners and counsel have become a major part of the organizational and compensation structure of most major firms, excluding the Elite Firms, and the source of significant additional profits for equity partners.

Law firms have also created new categories of less well-compensated lawyers that fall outside of the traditional partner, nonequity partner, counsel, and associate categories such as career and contract associates, some of whom work in less expensive locations in the United States and abroad and whose utilization is facilitated by advances in Internet and telephonic communications.

(b) Billable Legal Service Providers Who Are Not Lawyers

One of the most important changes in law firm operations over the last 40 years has been the growing use of legal service personnel who are not licensed lawyers, but whose work is billed to clients. Law departments have also increased their reliance on unlicensed personnel in order to reduce the cost of licensed lawyers in their operations.

Of the four types of nonlawyer billable legal service personnel functioning in the United States today, only one to date has contributed significantly to the creation of the modern major business practice law firm or law department—legal assistants. Personnel in this established group (often referred to as paralegals) provide their legally related services under the supervision of lawyers in their firms or law departments. As we will see, while all paralegals are legal assistants, not all legal assistants are paralegals because some provide chargeable services that are not inherently legal in nature.

The other three categories of nonlawyer legal service providers currently functioning in the United States include 1) *notaries public* who have long played a role in providing legal services in the State of Louisiana, 2) the relatively new category of *alternative legal service providers* or *ALSPs*, and 3) *paralawyers* such as those newly introduced in the State of Washington. More information about notaries public, ALSPs and paralawyers will be found in Chapter Seven, *The Future of the Legal Profession*, and in Chapter Eight, *Alternative Legal Service Providers and Paralawyers*.

In the early 1970s, in part because of the Viet Nam War, many firms were unable to find the associate level assistance they needed to respond to growing client needs. Some realized that not all of the work their well-compensated young associates were doing required a standard legal education. At the same time clients were becoming unhappy with the high hourly rates charged for inexperienced young lawyers. One answer was for law firms to employ paralegals whose services could be billed to clients, but who were not licensed attorneys.

In due course it occurred to law firms that some of the work done by their secretaries was similar to chargeable work being done by their paralegals, and that they could charge for some of their secretaries' time if the secretaries had a somewhat different job description and title. Initially, doing so was complicated because much of the work performed by secretaries continued to be "pure secretarial work" like taking dictation, typing documents, and maintaining files, which were not considered to be legal services.

However, as computers led to lawyers doing their own typing, editing, and electronic record keeping, "secretarial work" diminished and lawyer and paralegal billable time increased. In due course, it became possible to classify some secretaries' time as paralegal work that could be billed to clients, and the distinction between legal secretaries and paralegals blurred. Law firms began to reduce the size of their secretarial staffs and enlarge their paralegal staffs—in the process converting some previously non-billable work to billable work. In addition, lawyers doing their own typing and electronic filing were spending some time on clients' work previously spent by secretaries which has increased lawyers' billable hours.

Initially, clients welcomed the reduction in cost resulting from the utilization of paralegals doing some of the work that otherwise would have been done by more expensive associates. Paralegal hourly rates have continued to rise along with increases in lawyer hourly rates.

When firms began experimenting with the paralegal concept there were few formal training programs available, and most of the training was on the job. But in due course, paralegal schools developed as women (and a few men) without law degrees sought the opportunity to work as paralegals without first serving as secretaries.

As this phenomenon grew the ABA decided to exercise some control over paralegal education. In August 1973, the House of Delegates of the Association adopted the Guidelines for the Approval of Legal Assistant Education Programs which had been proposed by its Special Committee on Legal Assistants, and the Committee subsequently developed evaluative criteria and procedures for obtaining ABA approval. The first applications to approve such programs were accepted in the fall of 1974.

Eventually public junior colleges (now often designated community or technical colleges) and for-profit vocational schools added programs to train interested individuals in some of the required paralegal skills. The curricula for the schools approved by the ABA required courses on such topics as Paralegal Ethics and Professional Responsibility, Legal Research and Writing, Civil Procedure and Litigation, Advanced Civil Procedure and Litigation, and then elective courses in areas such as Family Law, Wills, Probate and Estate Administration, Business Organizations and Contracts, Bankruptcy, Torts, Labor and Employment Law, and Real Property Law.

During the same period state bar associations began to take note of the use of paralegals and adopted rules to govern their use. Advisory Opinion 21 of the State Bar of Georgia, initially issued in September of 1977, deals with "Guidelines for Attorneys Utilizing Paralegals." It notes, ironically, that because paralegals are not lawyers, the bar has no jurisdiction over them, but it has jurisdiction over lawyers and law firms using paralegals to provide legal services, and specifies how they could and could not be appropriately used.

The key concept with respect to paralegals is that a lawyer may delegate "activities which ordinarily comprise the practice of law" to "clerks, secretaries and other lay persons," but the lawyer must maintain a direct relationship with the client, supervise the delegated work, and take complete professional responsibility for the work product. This is the most sensitive part of the lawyer-legal assistant concept. It requires not only that the lawyer oversee the paralegal's work, but also that the lawyer maintain a direct relationship with the client." Exactly what constitutes a "direct relationship" is unclear.

It is important that law firms employing paralegals supervise their work to be sure that they are complying with all applicable ethical, professional and legal obligations such as maintaining confidences and working with ordinary skill. It would be desirable that a firm have a contract with each of its paralegals specifying their responsibilities, their agreement to comply with all firm protocols for the work performed and to abide by the firm's rules, practices and procedures, including all ethical and professional rules applicable to them. Under typical state bar rules, the supervising attorney has a duty to actually review the work and assure that it meets the firm's standards.

The extent to which paralegal work is supervised by lawyers within their firms depends on the capability and tenure of the paralegal employees and the appetite of equity partners for additional work and profits. Supervised or not, errors in the performance of their work remain the responsibility of their firms. It should be noted that the rules are silent with respect to charges to clients for paralegal services.

The rules do not on their face address the use of paralegals in-house, and if so used, how supervised. Businesses are unlikely to sue themselves over their own legal assistant's unlicensed practice of law, but they presumably could sue one of their lawyer-employees for inadequate supervision of a department paralegal whose work results in a loss to their employer. In addition, third parties such as trustees in bankruptcy proceedings might want to pursue in-house lawyers if they improperly relied on paralegals in a way that led to a loss of company resources. For this reason law departments may want to carry lawyer malpractice insurance to protect their individual lawyers and their employers.

Once it became established that paralegals working under the supervision of lawyers could provide services in connection with the delivery of legal services, and that clients could be billed for such services and would pay for them, the way was open for firms to add a wide variety of other categories of legal assistants as nonlawyer billable service providers. Some of these legal assistants provide services that would not be considered *legal work* including investigation, contract administration, construction consulting, scientific advice and others.

Professor William Henderson of the Indiana University School of Law believes that a diamond shaped law firm profile is replacing the dominant pyramid structure of the last several decades with a larger group of counsel and nonequity partners in the middle, supported in turn by a smaller number of associates, rather than the deleveraged profile predicted by Professor Richard Susskind.

Despite the growing number of middle rank lawyers and the decline in the number of regular associates, I believe a restructured law firm pyramid still exists in most major law firms with growing numbers of billable legal assistants of various sorts as well as contract and leased lawyers taking the place of many of the expensive associates that in the past have constituted the base of the pyramid.

In retrospect, the extensive utilization of legal assistants has been one of the most significant developments in the delivery of legal services in the United States since the end of World War II. It introduced, and over time validated, the use of unlicensed billable employees to support lawyers in providing the legal services of law firms and in law departments, and has enabled law firm partners to profit from the work of unlicensed nonlawyer legal service providers.

Many firms have expanded their employment of a variety of billable nonlawyer personnel. In some firms these billable nonlawyer employees constitute 20% or more of their total billable personnel.

Below are two graphs that illustrate the changes that have occurred in the personnel make-up of many major firms over the last 55 years. While the graphs are based on information available to me about the Atlanta market, I believe they represent fair approximations of the nature and scale of the changes that have occurred in many major firms throughout the United States. These changes vary to some degree from region to region and firm to firm, and some firms have taken a different path.

CHANGES IN THE DEMOGRAPHICS OF MAJOR LAW FIRMS 1960—2015

PERCENTAGE OF FIRM PERSONNEL IN VARIOUS CATEGORIES INCLUDING NONLAWYER BILLABLE AND NONBILLABLE SUPPORT STAFF

1960

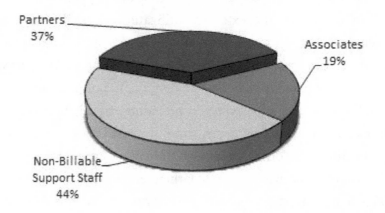

Partners 37%

Associates 19%

Non-Billable Support Staff 44%

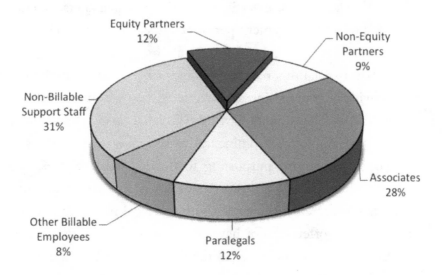

The 2015 graph above does not take into account contract or leased lawyers who normally do not appear in publically available listings of law firm personnel and represent another significant layer of leverage supporting equity partner compensation.

The realization over recent decades that *very good* legal services are often good enough and that some services do not require highly trained and expensive lawyers has empowered law departments to use the services of law firms and ALSPs utilizing less expensive lawyers and nonlawyer personnel, and to increase their own utilization of legal assistants.

While paralegals are the largest part of this growing group of nonlawyer billable employees, the group also includes many other categories of legal assistants such as case assistants, construction consultants, contract administrators, data analysts, discovery specialists, docket clerks, investigators, litigation managers, pricing specialists, project management personnel, researchers, and scientific advisors.

State bar associations receive hundreds of complaints each year about individuals and businesses practicing law without a license. Ironically, the state bars do not have legal jurisdiction over nonlawyers and therefore cannot take administrative action against unlicensed persons or organizations purporting to provide legal services. In many states the unauthorized practice of law is a misdemeanor and the state law enforcement agencies with the legal power to enforce malpractice laws often do not have the personnel or motivation to pursue these law breakers. In 2013 the State of New York increased many of the penalties for the unauthorized practice of law to the felony level.

Anyone providing incorrect legal advice, whether they are properly licensed or not, may be called to account. We can expect to see a good deal more debate and litigation surrounding the troublesome issues of "what is the practice of law" and "where it is being practiced."

Most law schools have ignored the legal assistant phenomenon. They have surrendered the opportunity to participate in the training of legal assistants to junior colleges and vocational schools. Now that many law schools have more faculty and facilities than they require for their present and prospective law school enrollments, some may want to encourage the creation of legal assistant and paralawyer education programs within their parent universities and to participate in them.

As we will see in Chapters Seven and Eight the legal assistant phenomenon in due course paved the way for the alternative legal service provider phenomenon of recent years.

(7) TECHNOLOGY

A seventh factor, technology, also has had a significant effect on the delivery of legal services worldwide and on the structure of what we now call the legal services industry. Four types of technology have been particularly transformative: communications technology, document creation and review technology, knowledge management technology, and project management technology.

The Internet, e-mail and video calls/conferencing have almost eliminated the barriers of distance and time between lawyers, their clients and other people with whom lawyers deal. Virtual reality developments may entirely eliminate barriers of distance in the next generation. These communications technologies have made it possible for lawyers anywhere to connect with clients and related parties everywhere, and have fundamentally altered the way in which lawyers and their clients communicate.

As a result, proximity is less important to clients today in the selection of their legal advisors than it has been at any time in our history. Today lawyers often provide legal services remotely to clients they have only met over the Internet or telephone. As a result, most potential clients in the USA are now fair game for any law firm in any city in the United States, and for other English-speaking lawyers wherever they reside (subject to jurisdictional licensing restrictions that are seemingly becoming less important except with respect to court appearances).

Advances in communication technology have also enabled law firms and law departments to relocate some of their costly administrative services from high-cost centers like New York City and San Francisco to less expensive towns like Wheeling, West Virginia and Nashville, Tennessee. In some cases state and local governments have provided tax deferrals and other benefits to law firms relocating jobs to their communities.

Since the early 1990s there has been a growing use of electronic communications and the easy creation of electronic documents that has led to a vast increase in the amount of business communications and of documents created and retained. Document review in litigation and corporate due diligence reviews had historically been provided by junior associates, and it was natural to continue to use their services to review and cull this enlarged body of communications and documents. It was also very profitable to the law firms doing the work.

In due course some law firms realized that they could profitably perform parts of their document review work by hiring less expensive lawyers often utilizing contract or leased lawyers. Eventually, law departments realized that they could send such work directly to lower-cost providers, aggregate the finished products into an appropriate response, and reduce their costs in the process. Much of it today is being done by computer aided predictive coding. The re-sourcing of this work and the increasing use of computers and increasingly sophisticated software tools have taken away some of the financial windfall for law firms that technology had created in the first place.

Despite the utilization of ALSPs, the off-shoring of some of this work to lower cost jurisdictions, and the use of predictive coding, the costs of document review work remain considerable. It has been estimated that the market for e-discovery services in 2019 will be $14.7 billion.

Technology has also enabled the creation of new document and project management systems. These software tools facilitate the creation, standardization and utilization of documents and may reduce the time and cost required to manage some legal projects, and in some cases may increase them. Technology has not only enabled many lawyers to improve the quality and efficiency of their services, but it has also resulted in longer and more complex documents. As a result, more time and attention is required to analyze and understand these documents which adds to the cost of their production and utilization.

In the days when typewriters were used to create documents, and copies had to be made by use of carbon paper (unless a commercial printer was used to set the documents in type), long documents and multiple changes were anathema to lawyers. Typing (especially making carbon copies) was a much slower and more complicated process than using computers and high-speed printers. If changes were made on the beginning pages of a document, the entire document had to be retyped. Errors had to be corrected individually on each copy. Consequently, documents were shorter and fewer changes were made. Computerized word processing and high-speed copy machines changed all of that, and essentially eliminated the constraints that had favored short documents and few changes, and reduced the need for concise and precise documents. Thankfully, an emerging trend stemming from newer consumer-facing regulations such as EU data privacy rules are beginning to counter this trend with requirements for simpler or plain language.

Document assembly software and work flow tools have enabled law firms and law departments to quickly prepare and alter standard contracts for use by their clients.

Knowledge management tools have made it possible for lawyers to access vast quantities of legal knowledge and know-how. These tools are readily available to any lawyer, law firm or law department willing and able to pay the cost of access, some of which would not have been available to them in the past. This expanded access has greatly strengthened the ability of 1) law departments to serve their employer-clients with less assistance from private practice firms, 2) new and new model law firms to compete with established firms, and 3) established firms to compete against one another.

It is important to note however, that such knowledge management programs do not add significant value to the work of lawyers with a rigorous subject matter specialization (today including many BigLaw partners). Such specialists already know the relevant laws, precedents and literature in their jurisdiction relating to their areas of specialization; they only need to check on possible new developments. That is a primary benefit of specialization.

On the other hand, access to such knowledge management tools is helpful to lawyers who are not specialists in the subject at hand, and therefore should also be helpful to smaller firms and solo practitioners with a broad practice who become skilled in computer aided research.

Technology law is itself becoming a larger and more important legal specialty contributing to the increasing size and complexity of the body of American and international law.

While technology has enabled the more cost-effective delivery of legal services, it has also added the countervailing costs of acquiring new hardware and software, and training firm lawyers and other personnel in their use. New equipment, software programs and training are not inexpensive.

I have deliberately avoided the use of the popular buzzword of the day–*disruptive technology*. All important new technology changes the way we do things. Most of the changes force us to adapt, and we would not do so if the changes were not helpful. Most of the new technology available to practicing lawyers has assisted and improved the practice of law rather than interrupting or disturbing such efforts. High-speed printers, computers, word processing and other software, and the Internet have aided the practice of law rather than disrupting it.

The effects of technology on lawyers, law firms and law departments are significant and enduring, and will continue to drive change in the legal profession in the future.

As a result of these fundamental changes in legal services over the last seventy years, the legal profession as we know it today is very different from the profession that emerged from World War II. Most present day lawyers are unaware of the many significant changes that have occurred or of the effects that such changes have had on the delivery of legal services today.

The continuing evolution of the practice of law in response to changing economic, technological, and cultural developments has been so gradual and prolonged that the magnitude and significance of these changes has been missed by many. Each new generation of lawyers takes for granted what they find in place, and measure change against their beginning point. As a result, they often exaggerate the magnitude and significance of anticipated changes which seem disproportionately important if they are not viewed within the context of the ongoing longer-term transformation of the practice of law.

CHAPTER THREE

The Present

TODAY'S LAW PRACTICE ENVIRONMENT

The Great Recession interrupted the growth of many major business practice firms and the growing enrollment in American law schools. Advances in technology and new service providers continue to drive change in the process of providing legal services. Many law firms are concerned about their own prospects, the strategies they should adopt and their chances of survival. There continue to be many lateral moves and mergers, as well as some law firm closures. Law firm mergers are at an all-time high, and are sometimes a convenient way of restructuring what otherwise would have been a failed law firm; they are often accompanied by immediate or short-term personnel changes and practice area adjustments.

U.S. lawyers are accustomed to seeking answers to current issues by referring to the past, in part because U.S. law (excepting Louisiana's) is based on the English common law which in turn is based to a great extent on precedential decisions rather than on codified law. We are accustomed to following an established path rather than moving in a new direction.

Unfortunately, the pace of transformation is rapid and the risk of not adjusting is great. As a result, most firms do not have the luxury of waiting until the path to future success has become clear before deciding what to do next. Borrowing large amounts of money to span a downturn or to fund a transformation or restructuring have proved hazardous for many firms including Dewey and Howrey.

My 2012 book, *Declining Prospects*, identified five developments that continue to adversely affect the economics of many law firms in America. I will not undertake here to repeat all of what I said there, but the following summary describes the present status of the economics of the legal profession in the United States.

Competition in the legal world is still increasing because of 1) an excess supply of capable lawyers and law firms, and the increasing presence of alternative legal service providers, 2) the high cost of legal services, 3) the growing capability of in-house law departments, 4) standardization, commoditization and disaggregation, and 5) technology.

SATURATING THE MARKET

The population of the United States grew from 150,697,000 in 1950 to 320,091,000 in 2015, an increase of approximately 112 percent. During the same period of time the number of lawyers in the United States increased from 221,600 to 1,301,000, an increase of approximately 487 percent. As a result we now have one lawyer for every 246 Americans compared to one for every 680 Americans in 1950. Then as now many licensed lawyers are not practicing law.

As a point of comparison, there are about 930,000 doctors in the United States today or approximately one for every 344 Americans. It has been estimated that by 2025 there will be a doctor shortage of 90,000 in the USA.

There were 206 ABA-accredited law schools in the United States in the fall of 2015, and 37,058 first year students enrolled in them, a decline of almost 30% from the peak in 2010 of 52,488 first-year students. The 2015 first year class was the smallest since the fall of 1973 (43 years ago) when there were 55 fewer accredited law schools. Obviously some law schools have been downsized.

The graduating class of 2015 was 39,984 and only about 67% found full-time jobs requiring a law degree within 10 months of their graduation. An additional 14.5% had found jobs for which a JD degree provided an advantage but was not a requirement, and an additional 5.6% were employed in other capacities.

It is difficult to reconcile the ABA's number of licensed lawyers with the Bureau of Labor Statistics' number of employed lawyers. In any event the Bureau has projected that the US economy would produce a total of about 157,700 jobs for lawyers between 2014 and 2024 due to growth and replacements, of which 43,800 would be additions to the lawyer workforce, and the remainder would be replacements for lawyers who retire, die or otherwise cease practicing law.

If law schools continue to produce graduates at the current pace there would be many more new lawyers than would be jobs for them as lawyers, unless there is considerable growth in the number of practicing attorneys that leave the workforce. This prediction does not take into account the difficulty of predicting the full negative impact on law graduate employment of advances in technology and growth in the use of nonlawyer legal assistants and ALSPs.

The greatly increased supply of lawyers is a major contributor to the greatly increased competition among legal service providers. Competition has been increased further by the advent and growth of ALSPs, which have employed some of the law school graduates not employed by law firms or law departments. Even with recently reduced law school enrollments it is obvious that the supply of law school graduates is still increasing more rapidly than they can be absorbed into the profession.

COSTS

The aggregate cost of legal services has increased in recent years because of increased business activity, additional laws and regulations, changes in the way transactions and litigation are managed, and increased hourly rates. The total cost to businesses for their legal services has been growing by leaps and bounds. Evidence of this increase can be found in the gross revenues of the top 50 Am Law 100 firms which grew from $3.4 billion in 1985 to $60.77 billion in 2015; an increase of more than 1,680% during a period of time when inflation had been approximately 120%. Adjusted for inflation the $3.4 billion of costs in 1985 would have been $7.5 billion in 2015 rather than $60.77 billion. Each of the top 27 firms in gross revenue in 2015 collected more than $1 billion in fees and the top five firms each collected more than $2 billion.

These numbers do not include the costs of the law departments of businesses, governments and not-for-profit organizations which have grown during this period of time in an effort to manage the growth in legal expenses.

LAW DEPARTMENTS

The most important competitors of private practice law firms are law departments. These departments have grown greatly in number and importance over the last four decades. The principal goals of organizational law departments are to achieve very good results, to improve the coordination of legal services and organizational operations, and to control or reduce legal costs.

As legal issues have become ubiquitous in the operation of modern organizations and as legal costs have increased, all but the smallest enterprises have concluded that they need some in-house legal service capability. In-house capability is necessary to reduce reliance on, and to manage relationships with, private practice firms. As in-house lawyers become more knowledgeable about their employers' operations they can more cost-effectively identify and address the issues within their range of responsibilities. Most law departments have found that there are plenty of capable lawyers willing or preferring to work in-house.

The growth of organizational law departments in capability, size, responsibility and confidence has been one of the most important changes in the legal profession in America in recent decades. The key point is that many law departments have become both knowledgeable and competent *suppliers* of legal services to their employers and, when necessary, knowledgeable and competent *buyers* of legal services from private practice firms and alternative legal service providers. Law departments are growing in size and capability, and their need for outside legal assistance has stabilized or is declining. Consequently, private practice lawyers and firms at all levels will continue to be under pressure to become more cost-effective providers of legal services.

Nonetheless, as law departments have grown, private practice law firms have grown even more as a result of the increasing overall demand for legal services.

STANDARDIZATION AND DISAGGREGATION

The growing use of document assembly systems and nonlawyer personnel to manage transactions has made it necessary to standardize many commercial relationships. Standardization has become a necessary part of the efficient operation of organizations that have found they cannot afford to have a lawyer standing by to assist operating personnel with routine transactions.

Some projects in their entirety are standard services. However, large and complex projects are more likely to involve a variety of services, some of which are routine and others not. Law departments are increasingly likely to disaggregate legal projects by retaining routine and recurring work which they take on themselves or outsource to less expensive service providers, and outsourcing to law firms projects (or parts of projects) too large for the department to handle or requiring highly specialized skills and experience not available in-house.

TECHNOLOGY

The contributions of technology to increased competition among lawyers, law firms and law departments have already been discussed in Chapter Two as one of the important factors driving change in the legal profession.

The preceding five factors—the growing number of capable lawyers and law firms; high legal services costs; the growth in size and capability of law departments; standardization, commoditization and disaggregation; and technology—coupled with their persistent interaction—are continuing to drive change in the legal services industry today, and will continue to do so in the future.

WHAT STRATEGY?

What strategies will law firms adopt in order to deal with the changing legal services landscape?

Law firms have rarely attempted to plan their futures more than a few years ahead and have tended to focus on practical considerations rather than on strategy. Today more lawyers and law firms are trying to find a strategy to guide their future operations that will permit them to stabilize or improve their economic position and preserve their firms.

The wide-spread confusion over strategy is not surprising given the complexity involved in identifying and implementing a successful one. Among the issues that every sizable firm must address in developing its strategy are:

Expertise Levels

Geographic Coverage

Knowledge & Know-how Management

Legal Service Offerings

Marketing Strategy

Office Locations

Personnel Composition & Utilization

Pricing Model

Profit sharing

Profitability Objectives

Project Management

Quality & Risk Control

Size

Specialization

Support Programs & Personnel

Technology & Systems Utilization

With such a variety of issues it is easy to see how difficult it is to change successfully an existing firm or to create a successful new firm. Among the models that have emerged are: firms that provide top-level expert advice, firms that specialize in one or limited areas of practice, diversely capable medium and large local or regional firms, diversely capable very large national or international firms, economy service firms, unleveraged firms, virtual firms, and small local firms. It is really not possible for a single firm to successfully and profitably do everything that every client requires.

BigLaw—Competition among the Major Firms

A popular buzzword with the legal press these days is "BigLaw." It is a phrase intended to encapsulate the major law firms in the USA and those in the UK with a major US presence (though given recent contractions due to the anticipated British exit from the EU the prospect of changes in this grouping are possible). BigLaw would certainly include the Am Law 100 firms and probably the Am Law 200 as well. Firms qualify for these listings based on their Gross Revenues.

In 2015 the firm on the Am Law 100 list with the largest gross revenue was Latham & Watkins with $2.65 billion of gross revenues, 2,177 lawyers, 454 equity partners and 176 nonequity partners. DLA Piper, Baker & McKenzie, Skadden, Kirkland & Ellis, Jones Day, Sidley Austin, Morgan Lewis, Hogan Lovells, and Norton Rose Fulbright rounded out the top ten. During 2015, Dentons grew to become the largest affiliated group of lawyers in the world with over 7,000 attorneys.

Only one of the 10 firms with the most gross revenue in 2015 (Kirkland) was among the 10 firms most profitable for their equity partners. Indeed, the firm with the highest profits per partner (Wachtell Lipton) was 37th on the gross revenue list, and the second ranked firm in profits per partner (Quinn Emanuel) was 26th. The firm ranked 6th on the PPP list (Cravath) was 50th on the gross revenue list and the firm ranked 8th (Cahill) ranked 85th on the gross revenue list. It's obvious that a successful "profits strategy" is different from a "gross revenue strategy" and that some BigLaw firms are significantly different from others.

The financial success of a law firm for its partners has less to do with the law firm's size and leverage than with the type of legal work they do, how long and how well they have been doing it, and how well they work together as a team. There is no discernable correlation between size and leverage on one hand and equity partner profitability on the other. Most of the largest firms and many highly leveraged firms are less profitable for their equity partners than some of the smaller and less leveraged firms. Consequently, it is a mistake to think of the Am Law 100 firms as though they were all in the same class.

THE ELITE FIRMS

In fact there is a much smaller group of firms included within the Am Law 100 that are in a class of their own that I refer to as the "Elite Firms." The Elite Firms are in a class by themselves because of their significant differences from most of the other firms in the Am Law 100. Their firm reputations transcend the reputations of their individual partners. Their lawyers share their firm's accumulated knowledge and know-how, and their firms remain the focus of their efforts rather than their individual agendas and reputations. As a result, their collective resources are available to all of their clients and exceed the knowledge and resources that any one partner or groups of partners could bring to the table in a firm where partners have an incentive to hoard their knowledge and know-how rather than share it with their colleagues.

My criteria for selecting such firms focuses on four characteristics—they have 1) only equity partners, 2) lock-step compensation (or a close approximation thereof), 3) no or very few lateral partners (excluding the initial organizers of the firm or a few laterals from important government positions) and 4) sustained profitability as measured by Profits Per Partner of $2 million or more for each of the last six fiscal years.

Why do these factors make a difference between the firms that have them and other BigLaw firms? The Elite Firms are financially very successful firms that are really law firm partnerships rather than federations of lawyers and their practices. The absence of nonequity partners assures that the partners are all members of the same team, and the absence or very limited recruitment of lateral entry partners (for instance, Wachtell has added only four lateral entry partners in its 50+ years of existence) assures that all of the partners have been cooked in the same sauce; they have learned their trade in the same manner from the same instructors and are part of the same family.

The adhesion of the partnerships is further achieved by lockstep compensation (possibly with slight modifications) that rewards each of the partners for the success of the partnership as a whole and by generous pensions provided by the firms to their retired partners. Each active partner knows that his or her own pension will be dependent on the firm's continued profitability, and on maintaining such pensions for the existing retired partners. The $2 million PPP simply means that the firm has consistently been very successful financially.

Based on this criteria I believe there are 9 such firms headquartered in the United States, listed in the order of their 2015 PPP:

1) Wachtell Lipton
2) Paul, Weiss
3) Sullivan & Cromwell
4) Cravath
5) Simpson Thacher
6) Davis Polk
7) Skadden
8) Cleary Gottlieb
9) Debevoise

(I have placed Cravath in the Elite category despite its one nonequity partner because of a unique situation in which an equity partner stepped down to nonequity status to avoid a conflict with his spouse's governmental position (a single temporary exception to the firm's policy).

There were 11 other firms with PPP in excess of $2 million in each of the last 6 years that did not fit the criteria selected for the Elite Firms, some of which would view themselves as an elite firm and have reason to do so. Some of them have a higher PPP than some of the firms on my list. Most of those excluded have nonequity partners or do not have lockstep partner compensation systems. Some make a practice of recruiting lateral entry partners. In 2015 Kirkland had 405 nonequity partners, a number that exceeded its number of equity partners. Others have a significant number of lateral entry partners.

Each of the Elite Firms has only one class of partner (with the noted Cravath exception). They "breed their own" lawyers and rarely lose their partners to competitors, or resort to lateral hiring (excluding the addition of a very few partners from government and industry positions). None have been built on a lateral recruitment strategy.

Each has a strong capital base provided by their partners that has been created over the years and could finance their operations without bank borrowings. While they provide legal services on a national and international basis, all maintain their principal office in New York City; Wachtell maintains only one office and the others have four or fewer offices in the United States.

These firms are characterized first and most importantly by their experience, reliability, legal knowledge, legal know-how, proven good judgment, useful relationships, and by their many years of successful representation of clients in their fields of expertise. They focus intensely on selling knowledge and know-how rather than on fee volume, are relatively small in this day of behemoths, and have been very cautious in expanding. The two largest in 2015 were Skadden with 1,677 lawyers and Cleary with 1,203; the smallest was Wachtell with 261. The other six average 780 lawyers.

The Elite Firms have maintained their traditional pyramid structures which are an integral part of their process of training and developing top specialists for the future. They pay the highest starting compensation to their new associates (recently raised to $180,000 a year) and continue to attract highly-motivated top law school graduates from the top schools; they operate strong associate training and development programs and retain the best of their associates as partners.

Most of these firms have been among the elite American firms for generations. Five of the nine firms had their origins in firms founded in the 1800s, another was organized prior to World War II, two were organized shortly after the end of the War (one of which was an offshoot of an older major firm), and one in the 1960s.

The Elite Firms are highly profitable because their clients value highly the legal advice and service they provide, and they can charge for their services accordingly. They maintain a high level of profitability for all of their partners, and their partners feel fairly rewarded for their contributions to the firm's performance. Four of the firms (Wachtell,

Paul Weiss, Sullivan & Cromwell and Cravath) have enjoyed PPP of more than $3 million in each of the last six years.

The firm omitted from this list with the strongest claim to be included is Cahill Gordon which had a PPP in each of the six years of more than $3 million, but was omitted because it has continuously had a small number of nonequity partners (10 in 2015).

Some commentators have attributed high profitability to high leverage. The firm with the highest PPP, Wachtell Lipton, has an associate-partner leverage of 3.11 to 1. Cleary has the highest leverage in the group of 6.37 to 1. The average is 5.14 to 1. Many Am Law 100-200 firms that operate with the same or more leverage are unable to generate the same top-level PPP.

It is almost impossible for a firm to pull itself up by its boot straps to join the ranks of the Elite Firms. No firm created in the last 50 years has been able to do so. Consequently for these various reasons the Elite Firms are advantaged over their many competitors. They have earned their reputations over substantial periods of time as the leading firms in the United States and are among the international elite as well.

Most of the other BigLaw firms are trying to catch up with the Elite Firms. It is more likely that one of the Elite Firms will falter than that a non-elite Firm will join the Elite fraternity.

THE REMAINDER OF BIGLAW

Most major firms want to do more of the most demanding and highly-profitable legal work and are competing with one another for such business that has not already been secured by the Elite Firms. There are basically two ways to qualify for such work. They must enhance and maintain their firm's knowledge, expertise and reputation, and effectively market its capabilities, or they must acquire lawyers or groups of lawyers who already have such expertise, reputation and clientele.

The development of enhanced expertise and reputation internally is difficult and usually requires a long timeframe of consistent effort; some luck helps. Expertise and reputation can be acquired only by sorting out the law and related issues in real transactions. Getting an assignment that could provide such expertise is often difficult and may require the sacrifice of both time and profit. If obtained it may not result in the desired objective. There are always skeptics among the partner ranks who do not want to reduce their own current income to fund someone else's effort to enhance their individual reputation and skills. If the effort proves to be successful, the lead partner or partners in the effort may undertake to retain control of the benefits of the representation within their existing firm, or by creating a new firm, or moving to another.

LATERAL MOVES

The other principal alternative is to acquire lawyers who are currently working for other firms who already have substantial legal business and relationships that they think they can move to another organization, and who have the expertise and reputation to retain and attract additional profitable legal work. Partners "controlling" significantly profitable business are in great demand, and the lateral acquisition of such partners remains the number one strategy of most Am Law 200 firms (but not the Elite Firms). The bruising competition for clients, which has led to a frenzy of lateral hiring, continues to be a major factor destabilizing many major firms and motivating many mergers.

Lateral partners who are able to move because of a good client base and/or expert knowledge and experience often are reluctant to share their clients and their knowledge with their new colleagues because the lateral's clients and knowledge are the basis of the lateral's economic advantage. Many laterals tend to pursue their personal interests more than their new firm's interests, and they frequently are not fully integrated into their new firms. (The lateral's move may have been motivated in the first place by the desire to obtain a greater share of the benefits of his experience and relationships.) Once partners have moved from one firm to another in order to obtain a better deal, they are more likely to make another such move that promises to further enhance income and standing. These difficulties are reflected in the fact that only about 35 percent of lateral moves are deemed to be successful by the acquiring firms.

The legal profession's outdated "free-market/lateral move" policy is damaging the profession and its ability to serve the needs of clients. Lateral moves are a major distraction that have often been destabilizing for firms losing partners and upsetting to firms gaining them.

Some lateral moves have been arranged through a process that almost certainly violated the agency law obligation of loyalty that all lawyers have to their current law firms, and in some cases may have involved the acquiring firms in inappropriate activities as well. In the current laissez-faire environment, many lawyers appear to have forgotten that as agents they have a fiduciary obligation of loyalty to their principals (which they should have learned in their first year course in agency).

As a result, I think that the strategy of growing by lateral hiring will become more difficult and less desirable as the injured firms assert their legal rights in order to retain their valuable clientele. It should be unnecessary to note that law firm clients are clients of the firm representing them, not of their individual partners; that's part of what engagement letters are about. The performance of work under an engagement letter is the responsibility of the firm and the firm is responsible if it is not performed properly.

All lawyers (partners or employees) as agents of their firms have a fiduciary duty of loyalty to their firm until their agency has been terminated. Without the firm's permission, it is a breach of fiduciary duty for them to discuss with a firm client the transfer of the client's legal business to another firm.

Because of the difficulties involved in upgrading a firm's expertise and capabilities by either hard work or lateral hiring most of the larger non-elite firms will find it very difficult to acquire the most challenging and profitable legal work, and as a result to acquire the required knowledge, expertise, relationships, and reputation. They will also have to compete on price and service.

CONTINUING CHANGE

There is a rationalization process under way in BigLaw involving many mergers, lateral moves and legal personnel shifts as firms seek to find the best configuration and model in the changing world of legal services. Ninety-one law firm mergers occurred during 2015, and an additional 21 law firm mergers were completed during the first quarter of 2016. The smaller firm in two-thirds of the mergers had five to 20 lawyers, and in one-third of the mergers the smaller firm had 21 to 100 lawyers. Dentons' recent expansion, which has involved eight mergers in 2015 alone, produced a behemoth of more than 7,000 lawyers with some 125 offices located in countries around the world.

I believe that we will see many more law firm "mergers" as well as many lateral moves of attorneys from one firm to another, and that many firms will shrink, merge or fail as work continues to move in-house and as competition becomes more intense.

As clients with law departments have become more experienced and sophisticated *buyers* as well as *providers* of legal services, they have realized that they hold the trump card in most situations and can pay less to obtain very good legal services. Clients are increasingly demanding more value at a lower price—a price comparable to what they would pay to staff the work in-house—and many capable lawyers and law firms are responding to such demands. There is no shortage of competition.

Some law department lawyers do not relish hard-nosed negotiations with their outside counsel over fee arrangements. This problem has been solved by some law departments by turning such negotiations over to their company's procurement department, or at least by involving their pricing specialists in the process.

At the same time ALSPs are continuing to syphon off some of the work that has been very profitable for major firms, as well as some of the work that has been the bread and butter of smaller firms.

Consequently, the prospects of continuing the recent highly profitable practice of law are declining for many firms. The few Elite Firms with the greatest knowledge, experience and reputation will continue to do very well financially, but many of the other Am Law 200 firms and smaller firms will not be able to identify and implement strategies that will upgrade their practice, and many will find new and less expensive alternative legal service providers competing in their market place.

DEVELOPMENTS ABROAD

The Legal Services Act of 2007 opened the door in England and Wales to Alternative Business Structures ("ABSs") thereby permitting other businesses including banks and retailers to provide legal services, and to enable nonlawyer investors in law firms. While ABSs do not have to be law firms or owned by lawyers, they still have to use members of the bar to provide Reserved Legal Services, and they will employ many lawyers as a result.

Some of the initial ABSs are focusing on high volume, low-value commodity work that is likely to attract individual clients more than businesses, and to compete with traditional small legal practices on convenience and cost. Some banks and other businesses may be comfortable offering corporate, conveyancing, probate, tax planning and trust services that are related to the services they normally provide, but I think it is much less likely that banks and retail businesses will undertake personal injury work or contract dispute resolution which would be inconsistent with their personnel and pricing practices, and the image they wish to convey to their customers.

The Reserved Legal Activities that constitute the practice of law in England and Wales are more narrowly defined than the practice of law in the United States. The six Reserved Legal Activities are: the exercise of rights of audience (i.e., appearing as an advocate before a court); the conduct of litigation (i.e., issuing proceedings before a court and commencing, prosecuting or defending those proceedings); reserved instrument activities (certain activities involving land registration and real property); probate activities; notarial activities; and the administration of oaths (i.e., taking oaths, swearing affidavits, etc.).

The Legal Services Act of 2007 also authorized the creation of multi-disciplinary practices ("MDPs") in England and Wales that could combine in one organization lawyers, accountants, independent financial advisors, estate agents, surveyors and other professional services providers. KPMG was the first of the Big Four accounting firms to register a MDP in England and Wales, and offers a variety of legal and law related services to its clients.

The Big Four accounting firms have been expanding their non-USA legal service capability and service locations in recent years. Deloitte Legal Services provides legal advice and support primarily to businesses in the banking, financial, insurance, real estate, energy, technology, and telecommunications industries in more than 70 countries. PwC is reported to have a legal network of 2,400 lawyers in 80 countries, and EY Legal has expanded its services to 64 countries in recent times.

These accounting firms are concentrating on areas of law that complement their existing services such as taxation, immigration, human-resource consulting, compliance, commercial contracts and due diligence. They are expanding their services in jurisdictions where they have a significant existing presence like China, Britain, Germany and Spain, and in other markets in which they currently have a presence and the large international law firms do not.

The latest twist in the ABS saga is the delivery of legal services to unrelated clients by corporate law departments. The law department of British Telecom has established as an ABS subsidiary, BT Law, which has its own board and management. It has been approved by UK regulators and is providing legal services to businesses, particularly with respect to high-volume claims and employment law.

While some law departments in the United States have undertaken to generate profits for their employer by identifying and pursuing claims against businesses infringing on their employer's intellectual property or failing to perform their contractual obligations, it had never occurred to me that law departments functioning through ABSs would offer legal services to unrelated third parties. It will be very interesting to see how the BT Law experiment works out.

The Canada Bar Association's "Legal Futures Task Force" released a report in 2014 supporting the concept of ABSs, and the Law Society of Upper Canada has authorized the creation of multi-disciplinary partnerships approved by the Society that may include professionals whose practice supports or supplements the practice of law or the provision of legal services, including accountants, tax consultants, and trademark and patent agents, etc.

Lawyers are no better or worse than other human beings in pursuit of high incomes in the 21st Century. Often, but not always, those best positioned to maximize their advantages have structured their firms in order to maximize their compensation. The most highly compensated partners in many firms take a disproportionate amount of the firm's profits because they have the power to do so. They have that power because, for whatever reason, they are able to attract and/or retain their firm's most profitable client business. Here again, many of the Elite Firms are an exception and operate with a different compensation plan.

CHAPTER FOUR

Predicting the Future of the Legal Profession

T he first three chapters of this book have been relatively easy to write—easy because they have described what has already occurred. Forecasting the future is more difficult.

The remarkable process of change that has taken place in the legal profession over the last 70+ years will continue in the future. We are witnessing and participating in an ongoing evolution of the legal services industry driven by 1) increased national and international economic and political activity, 2) the growing bodies of statutes and regulations necessary to manage such increased activity, 3) technology, and 4) increasing competition.

In order to focus on the future of the profession I have read widely in the available literature; I have discussed the principal issues with many knowledgeable lawyers, law firm leaders, and general counsel; I have made presentations at forums, conferences, and institutes; and I have participated in the give and take resulting from these events.

Needless to say, a great deal is being said and written on the subject by a growing cadre of consultants, academics and commentators. Some of it is uninformed and overwrought. If all of the adverse changes that had been predicted to occur in the legal profession over the last twenty years had occurred, the results would have been calamitous for many thousands of lawyers and law firms.

The leading legal futurist is British law professor and consultant, Richard Susskind, who is the preeminent prognosticator of the future of the legal profession in the English-speaking world. His analysis and predictions have been widely circulated in the United States and abroad. Some others who have joined in one aspect or another of the discussion and speculation (listed in alphabetical order) include Benjamin H. Barton, Casey Flaherty, Jordan Furlong, Steven J. Harper, William Henderson, Patrick J. Lamb, Paul Lippe, Bruce MacEwen, Patrick J. McKenna, Thomas D. Morgan, Aric Press, Judge John Toulmin, and David Wilkins.

In reaching my own conclusions about what the future holds for the legal profession I have considered the views of these experts and others while also taking into account my own study of the subject and my continuing daily experience as a practicing lawyer in a significant law firm confronting many of the issues facing the legal profession today.

FORESEEING THE FUTURE?

In order to accurately predict the future of the legal profession in the United States it is necessary to anticipate correctly the needs, activities and expectations of tomorrow's consumers of legal services. The needs will vary by major segments.

Individuals and families usually require legal services that relate primarily to property ownership and management, family relationships, elder law, healthcare, and administrative and criminal proceedings—services that are often provided by small firms and solo practitioners. Wealthy individuals and families are likely to seek more sophisticated advice from specialty firms for their estate planning and family law issues, and from major firms for their investment, property and business activities.

Organizations that need legal services include businesses (both privately and publically owned), governments (at local, regional, state, national and international levels), and not-for-profit organizations (foundations, charities, some educational institutions, some medical service providers, and others). The needs and requirements of these various legal service users vary significantly.

While the focus in the legal media is primarily on the major private practice firms and the law departments of for-profit businesses, the law departments and law firms representing governments and not-for-profit organizations are also major participants in the legal world.

Many small organizations rely largely or entirely on private practice lawyers and firms. Some may have a single in-house lawyer to manage their relationships with outside firms. Most medium-sized and larger organizations have law departments that provide many of the legal services they require and supervise the rest. Consequently, the most important legal service relationship for these organizations is with their own law department rather than with outside counsel.

Because some of the legal work for most legal service consumers is irregular or seasonal, private practice law firms (and/or alternative legal service providers) are retained to service the demand that exceeds normal in-house capacity. In addition to overflow work, if an issue requires a level of knowledge, know-how, experience, or relationship that is not available in-house, law departments often retain private practice lawyers and firms to provide what is needed.

In litigation clients utilizing counsel usually must be represented, at least in part, by a lawyer admitted to practice in the relevant jurisdiction. In addition, having local or specialized representation is frequently an advantage, if not a necessity, because of 1) differences in jurisdictional laws, rules, and procedures, 2) the importance of knowing local governmental processes, and 3) the potential advantage of using a lawyer with a working relationship with critical legal personnel such as administrators, judges, prosecutors, and their staffs.

In addition, clients whose continuing operations, or even their survival, are at risk will often retain expert firms to work with their in-house lawyers or their usual outside counsel in addressing such issues.

Clients continue to focus primarily on reducing their legal cost for very good service within our existing system, and this focus has been a major preoccupation of most commentators. There are continuing experiments with a variety of dispute resolution processes designed to supplement or substitute for the overloaded and often inefficient court systems. There is a growing concern that the growing body of law and regulation will be a permanent drag on economic activity.

PREDICTING THE FUTURE PRACTICE OF LAW

Predicting the evolving future of the practice of law and the legal profession has become a profitable occupation for law practice consultants and some law professors. But it is fraught with difficulty and uncertainty—such predictions have often been wrong.

Many large law firms and many law departments are investing millions of dollar to acquire technological support for, or alternatives to, established legal practices and functions. These investments in current and newly established facilities, equipment and software, as well as in the training of their personnel to utilize these new assets, are being made to maintain or reduce the cost of legal services to clients and to increase their profitability to law firms. They are often very expensive; if any of them fail, the investment in them would become a burdensome loss.

We do not yet know the full extent to which these investments might reshape the delivery and affect the cost of legal services, and in some areas of investment we do not know if the benefits to lawyers and/or their clients will offset the costs incurred to acquire them. The results of these efforts will affect the future operations and profitability of law firms and law departments, as well as the number and type of persons needed to provide legal services and the education and training they will require.

In addition, the success of alternative legal service providers inevitably will affect the prospects of traditional lawyers, law firms and law departments. Again, we do not know what the full effect will be. As firms seek to position themselves to serve the evolving needs of their clients, they will have to make reasoned guesses about the future needs of their existing and prospective clients, and about the capabilities of existing and new legal service providers.

CHAPTER FIVE

Professor Susskind's Predictions about the Last Twenty Years and the Future

Professor Richard Susskind is the most widely known and often quoted of the consultants and academic experts who have been speculating about the future of the legal profession during the last two decades. Many of the other commentators have followed his basic lead and echoed his prognosis. Consequently, I've chosen to concentrate on his predictions and will weave in other thoughts as may be appropriate from time to time.

Twenty years ago in his book, *The Future of Law*, Professor Susskind boldly predicted that by 2016 "many or most of our fundamental assumptions about legal service and legal process would be challenged and displaced by IT and the Internet." He further predicted that "legal service would move from being a one-to-one, consultative, print-based advisory service to a one-to-many, packaged, Internet-based information service."

In his 2013 book, *Tomorrow's Lawyers: An Introduction to Your Future*, Professor Susskind stood by his 1996 predictions:

> "Crucially, I concluded in 1996 that legal service would move from being a one-to-one, consultative, print-based advisory service to a one-to-many, packaged, Internet-based information service. I still think this—I believe it more strongly, in fact—and that is one premise upon which tomorrow's lawyers should build in planning for the long term."

He also stated in *Tomorrow's Lawyers* that:

> "I find it unimaginable that our current legal institutions and legal profession will remain substantially unchanged over the next decade. For much of the legal market, the model is not simply unsustainable, it is already broken."

And he predicted

> "that conventional lawyers will not be as prominent in society as today . . . . This prediction does not signal the end of lawyers entirely, but it does point to a need for fewer traditional lawyers."

He goes on to say that "the long-term prospects for most conventional lawyers are much more limited than in the past."

Now that 2016 is history, it is obvious that Professor Susskind's bold 1996 predictions were significantly wide of the mark! In essence he predicted 20 years ago that there would be a much reduced need for private practice lawyers by now; that many potential clients would no longer be in need of consultation with and advice from lawyers because they could obtain and make good use of most of the legal guidance they needed from information and forms available on the Internet.

While the legal profession has continued to evolve since 1996, many or most of our fundamental assumptions about legal service and legal process have not been displaced by IT and the Internet, and legal services are a long way from being a one-to-many, packaged, information service (on the Internet or otherwise).

With respect to large and highly leveraged firms Professor Susskind wrote in 2013 that:

> "[W]e will witness the end of leverage—at best the pyramid . . . will move from being broad-based to narrow-based."

> "[S]ome firms may strip away their junior and trainee lawyers, or stop recruiting them. They might operate with a team of high-powered partners, each supported by, say, one associate; and the routine work will be resourced beyond the firm."

The team he foresaw consisted of two kinds of lawyers; "expert trusted advisors" to assist clients with "high-value legal challenges," and technology savvy "enhanced practitioners" who will provide legal and technological support to expert trusted advisors. These categories correspond to the two categories of lawyers that he predicted would survive in his 1996 book, *The Future of Law*—legal specialists and legal information engineers.

In other words, Susskind foresaw the practice of law returning to the balance that existed at most firms during the 1950s and early 1960s when there were as many or more partners than associates in most law firms.

Although I expect the current very high levels of lawyer leverage that exists in many major firms will be reduced in the years ahead, I do not expect that leverage will recede to the levels that existed in most major American firms in the middle of the 20th Century. In addition, increasing numbers of legal assistants and career associates will supplement as well as replace some traditional associates. So there will continue to be personnel leverage but of a somewhat different kind.

In 2013 Susskind wrote with respect to medium-sized firms:

> "As for medium-sized firms, to survive and thrive I suspect most will need to merge and seek external investment to enable the changes from their current approach to a new, sustainable, longer-term business model . . . ."

> "I believe there will be a market for many years yet for small to medium-sized firms with demonstrable, niche expertise."

With respect to small firms he said:

> "As for much smaller firms with very few partners, aside from those which also offer a genuinely specialist or personal service that some market is prepared to pay for, I find it hard to imagine how these legal businesses will survive in the long run . . . . [B]anks and retailers will compete with sole practitioners and small firms for everyday legal services (such as conveyancing,

probate, and personal injury work). But it is likely that these alternative business structures . . . will standardize, systematize, and package legal services and bring cost savings, efficiencies, and experience that the traditional, small law firms will find impossible to match. This will be the end of lawyers who practice in the manner of a cottage industry. One person who formally reviewed my publication proposal for this book said that they hoped that I would pay more attention than in the past to general purpose small firms. I am afraid I was not inclined to do so, because I do not see much of a future (beyond 2020) for most small firms in liberalized regimes."

It would appear that Susskind does not see any significant advantages accruing to small firms or solo practitioners from the improvements in legal project and knowledge management software programs, in other new legal technologies, or in the utilization of legal assistants. I believe such support can breathe new life into small firms and enable them to survive and prosper.

Many of these technologies are expensive—a cost best shared by several lawyers. As a result, I agree that we will see fewer sole practitioners among the ranks of American lawyers, but I believe we will continue to have many small firms, some of which will use the capabilities of new technologies and new types of personnel to serve better the unserved and underserved end of the legal services market. The plaintiffs' bar, with many small firms, will also continue to benefit from the use of new technologies.

As will be discussed later, I expect to see opportunities develop for individual lawyers and small firms to offer their services on the premises of some banks and retail establishments.

Susskind has little to say about the changes he expects to occur in the size, scope and method of the operations of the law departments of businesses, governments and not-for-profit organizations that now represent a significant part of the legal profession. He does expect that law departments as well as law firms will employ some knowledge management and practice support lawyers in order to improve their efficiency.

Law departments will continue to perform the routine and frequently recurring work that is built into the legal system and business operations in the United States and most other countries, as well as taking on more of their employers' important legal work. Their services will be organized and executed to the extent possible utilizing software, computers, automation, and licensed and unlicensed personnel specifically trained for their jobs, as well as by alternative legal service providers (many utilizing law graduates to provide some of their services). Lawyers, inside or outside, will be required to oversee such work. Clients will not want their managers or their staff to look the law up on the Internet and to apply it as they see fit.

In the last chapter of *Tomorrow's Lawyers*, Susskind questions whether a closed and regulated legal profession is in the best interest of the public. He notes that our existing system is for many inaccessible and expensive. He also notes that the Internet would enable lay people to obtain legal guidance in the form of online legal guidance systems, automated document assembly systems, communities of legal experience, and through less costly consultation by video conferencing. Most of these systems and services have existed for a decade or more, and have been used and will continue to be used, but they have not produced the results that Professor Susskind has predicted for them.

He further states that the legal profession is a "closed shop" seeking to "preserve the problem to which they are the solution." He notes that the "jealous guards" within the profession work to "ring-fence areas of legal practice and make it their exclusive preserve, whether or not the activity genuinely requires the experience of lawyers and with little regard for the impact of this quasi-protectionism on the affordability and availability of legal services."

"Your elders will tend to be cautious, protective, conservative, if not reactionary. They will resist change and will often want to hang on to their traditional ways of working, even if they are well past their sell-by date."

I think Susskind's assessment of the status and future of the legal profession is unduly pessimistic. Because all lawyers are human beings there are among us some who are more oriented toward being "jealous guards" than "benevolent custodians." There are many of us in-between. The jealous guards are, with the consent and support of the legal profession, losing ground to technology, ALSPs, and legal assistants and paralawyers. For example, ALSPs like LegalZoom and Rocket Lawyer have seen the advantages of involving lawyers in the delivery of their services rather than fighting with them, and most of the state bar associations have acquiesced in their restructured operations.

Professor Susskind and his son Daniel appear to have upped their ante in a recent article appearing in the October 11, 2016 Internet edition of *Information & Technology, Harvard Business Review*, with the title *Technology Will Replace Many Doctors, Lawyers, and Other Professionals*. In the article they state their expectation "that within decades the traditional professions will be dismantled, leaving most, but not all, professionals to be replaced by less-expert people, new types of experts, and high-performing systems." They believe on one hand that many components of professional services "do not in fact call for "judgment, creativity or empathy," and on the other that "human professionals are already being outgunned by a combination of brute processing power, big data, and remarkable algorithms."

They cautiously hedge their prediction by the phrase "within decades" that could be far off in the future. It is not clear to me whether the Susskinds are thereby shelving for a few decades Professor Susskind's previous predictions, or otherwise restating his view of the future practice of law.

As noted earlier, Professor Susskind's predictions and analysis have been adopted to various degrees and repeated in various forms by many other academics and law practice consultants, and have become fashionable. But it is obvious that many of the fundamental changes Professor Susskind predicted to occur in the practice of law over the last twenty years have not occurred and seem unlikely to occur in the foreseeable future.

Despite his analysis, and in contradiction to his predictions, the number of lawyers in the United States has not diminished over the last 20 years; on the contrary, the number of lawyers in the USA has grown from 946,500 in 1996 to 1,301,000 in 2015 (an increase of about 37.5%).

I think it is too early in the 21st Century evolution of the practice to write-off lawyers and firms that are genuinely working to provide better and more cost-effective service to their existing clientele, as well as those trying to provide legal services to the underserved and unserved portions of the legal services market.

To be fair, predicting the future is always uncertain. I missed the mark 20 years ago in an important respect in *Profit and the Practice of Law*. While I accurately predicted the increase in specialization, the movement in-house of recurring legal work and excellent lawyers, the expulsion of *underperforming partners*, and the merger or collapse of some major firms, I thought that the decline in Profits Per Partner experienced in the early 1990s would continue. It didn't—I failed to foresee the growing use of leverage in the form of nonequity partners, career associates, leased associates, and billable nonlawyer personnel, and the relative reduction of equity partner ranks.

While I agree that change will continue, I do not see why we should expect the legal profession in the United States to change *beyond recognition* in the foreseeable future. Change is not really the issue; it is always with us. The issue is the type and rate of change that will occur, and how it will affect lawyers, law firms and law departments providing legal services, and clients needing their services.

Professor Susskind significantly overestimated the type and amount of change that would occur over the last 20 years and the impact of such changes on the demand for lawyers and legal services. And I think he continues to overestimate the amount of change likely to occur in the foreseeable future. The reasons why such changes have not occurred and are unlikely to occur are set forth in the next chapter.

CHAPTER SIX

Why Haven't Legal Services Become Information on the Internet?

Why have most legal services in the United States not become one-to-many, packaged, internet-based information services along the lines predicted by Professor Susskind in 1996? A great deal has happened since his predictions were initially made, but much of what he predicted has not occurred; to the contrary law departments and law firms have become larger and more numerous, many major law firms have become significantly larger and more profitable, and lawyer employment in the United States has increased by approximately one-third despite the effects of the Great Recession and the many changes occurring in the profession.

The principal reasons why many of the significant changes predicted by Professor Susskind have not occurred and why the legal profession has continued to grow in size and importance, are:

(1) The growing bulk and complexity of the law and legal systems, including the growing internationalization of many business and financial activities.

(2) The difficulty most people and organizations have in dealing with this bulk and complexity, even with the help of technology.

(3) Legal information alone in the hands of untutored individuals is rarely sufficient to cope successfully with legal issues.

(4) Much of the information now accessible on the Internet is not new—it has long been available in print—and hasn't made much difference in the demand for lawyer-provided legal services.

(5) The movement in-house of an increasing percentage of legal work (the work isn't disappearing, it's moving around).

(6) The need for know-how, experience and relationships to facilitate the legal process that generally are not available in books or on the Internet.

(7) The complex impact of technology, and

(8) The need of human beings for independent analysis and advice concerning many legal issues.

The practice of law has been a regulated and licensed profession for centuries in large part because most people have had difficulty coping with the complex legal issues and proceedings of their times and, in the absence of professional regulation and licensing, unscrupulous "advisors" have taken advantage of the unschooled and uninitiated public requiring assistance. The need for lawyers has grown as the complexity of our civilization has increased.

(1) INCREASING MAGNITUDE AND COMPLEXITY

Government and civilization are virtually synonymous; we look to governments to protect our lives, our property and our families, and to provide a fair and suitable means of resolving the inevitable disputes that arise. Modern society could not exist without the protections and services that governments provide.

The ever-increasing magnitude and complexity of laws, regulations, reported cases and other legal source materials is a result of the ingenuity and complexity of human nature, the unrelenting struggle between benevolent and malevolent forces, and conflicting claims by increasing numbers of people concerning the division of available assets.

Most of us are not saints, and we have an almost universal desire to increase our personal and family financial well-being. Laws and regulations and their interpretation and application significantly affect the lives and livelihood of everyone on the planet, and are the indispensable tools of governance. They will continue to increase in number and complexity.

One can reasonably dispute the necessity for, or the effectiveness of, many of our laws and regulations. We should applaud and encourage the search for improved approaches that might be less burdensome and more effective, but we could no more return to the level of governmental regulation that sufficed in the early days of our republic than we could provide for our national defense today with the same continental army and navy that we had in the 1780s.

Our country decided very long ago that we preferred the benefits of governments to the alternatives. Alexander Hamilton stated the case well when he wrote, "Why has government been instituted at all? Because the passions of man will not conform to the dictates of reason and justice without constraint."

One example of our increased legal complexity is the growth of the codified laws of the United States from a single large volume in 1926 to 41 volumes containing a total of 180,000 pages today.

Another measure of the significant increase in the volume and complexity of the law is the increased production of legal opinions by our courts. Between 1880 and 1924 (44 years) the Federal Courts of Appeal produced an average of 6.8 volumes of opinions a year. Between 1944 and 1993 (50 years) the Courts of Appeal produced an average of 14.5 volumes of opinions a year, and between 1993 and 2015 (22 years) the Courts of Appeal produced approximately 27 volumes a year—and the average length of opinions grew longer and the volumes thicker in each successive period.

A third example of increased complexity is the increased size of the United States' Internal Revenue Code and Regulations which have grown from 16,500 pages in 1969 to 74,608 pages in 2014.

The growing bulk of the law is not confined to our Federal Government; the laws and the regulations of the various states and the decisions of the state courts, as well as the ordinances and regulations of our counties and cities, have also become much more voluminous, as have the laws and regulations of other countries and international organizations. There are now 184 to 195 other independent nations of the world (depending on your criteria for independence) each with its own laws and regulations, and there is a growing number of international agencies and a growing body of international law that attempt to bring some order to international commerce, relations and disputes.

The paradox of technological advance is that instead of eliminating complexity it has made greater complexity possible, while helping us manage our increasingly complex and complicated world. Indeed, without the help of technology we might have already drowned in the complexity we have created. We should be glad for the help computers have provided, but they have contributed to increased complexity as well.

There will be a constant need to prune and modify overgrown or outdated local, state, national and international laws and regulations, and this continuing effort will also require the help of technology, a great many lawyers, and well-conceived plans.

Consequently, the demands on and the need for the legal system and the legal profession will continue to increase. Anyone who thinks that this growing complexity can be reduced and effectively managed by new technology with fewer lawyers is sadly mistaken.

Despite the frustration of many Americans with laws and regulations, no one has yet devised a workable way to avoid the creation of new laws and regulations or even to trim those that are no longer relevant or helpful. As our world becomes more complex, the fertile minds of entrepreneurs, business men and women, as well as con men and criminals, all now aided by computers and the Internet, will continue to seek to maximize their share of the economic pie, and governments will be expected to provide rational control and supervision. The key participants in this process have been and will continue to be lawyers.

(2) DIFFICULTY

Professor Susskind underestimates the difficulty the uninitiated public has in coping with legal issues, and he has overestimated the capacity of most people (including most well-educated people) to cope with the law and its administration on their own. I've seen many situations where clients thought they could manage an aspect of their legal affairs without a lawyer, but found the process more difficult and time consuming than they had anticipated or were able to tolerate. At issue is not just mental capacity and education—it is also available time, attention-span, conceptual familiarization, other distractions, as well as the relative importance of the matter at hand.

As one example, I recall two successful business men who were brothers initially rejecting an inexpensive proposal of the Alston firm to represent the estate of their recently deceased mother. They were quite confident that they could manage the process themselves without the assistance of lawyers and the related cost. A month later they returned to my office and literally "on bended knees" (done in jest) begged me to take the project off their hands. Many able people (and many others) do not have the time or attention span needed to cope with the law and the legal system.

Lawyers themselves often seek the assistance of other lawyers in addressing their own personal and financial legal issues that are outside their respective areas of expertise. It is hard for any of us to be objective and rational about matters that are very important to us. The truism attributed to Abraham Lincoln is obviously as true today as it was 150 years ago: "He who represents himself has a fool for a client."

As long-standing legal issues become understandable and manageable, new ones arise to take their place on the list of frustrating legal problems.

With respect to most of the legally unserved population, I believe they will continue to be unable to deal with their legal issues on their own even with the availability of relatively simple documents or proceedings. At a recent anniversary celebration of the Atlanta Legal Aid Society the audience heard stories of the assistance provided to previously unserved clients and the vital role that the Society's lawyers play in that process. No software or standardized form could in most cases have provided the legal support their indigent or nearly indigent clients required.

I think there is one significant part of the market for legal services (largely latent today) that may be able to use effectively some of the legal information and forms available on the Internet—underserved moderate income individuals, families and organizations. Educated individuals without sufficient income to employ a lawyer (or who have a preferred use for their money) may now more easily find information that may enable them to make an informed decision based on Internet information.

(3) DEALING WITH A LEGAL PROBLEM OFTEN REQUIRES MUCH MORE THAN LEGAL INFORMATION

Professor Susskind's basic mistake has been to think of legal service as an information service; it is much more than that. He has underestimated the fact finding, analytical, advisory and implementation aspects of legal services that are necessary to achieve a successful resolution of most legal issues. While legal information is an essential aspect of dealing with the law, it is the start rather than the finish of the legal process.

Personal computers can help find legal information which in simple cases may suffice as actionable legal advice, but for most legal situations the solution will require a factual and legal analysis, the application of the relevant law to the facts, the formulation of a plan of action and its implementation. The core of legal service is the amalgamation of factual and legal information, analysis, advice and action.

Personal computers and the Internet have increased and accelerated access to legal information, but the issue remains—do you have the right facts, do you have the right law, do you know what it means, and what do you do with the information once you have it? For instance, if you are an elderly person with a valid claim against a commercial bully, what can you do about it by yourself?

(4) MUCH OF THE INFORMATION NOW ACCESSIBLE ON THE INTERNET IS NOT NEW—IT HAS LONG BEEN AVAILABLE TO THE GENERAL PUBLIC IN PRINT.

For decades large amounts of legal source material and instructions have been available to the general public in the form of self-help publications, legal treatises and standard forms. Consider for a moment federal taxation—for decades the IRS has supplied the forms and there have been scores of high-quality books available about these laws and regulations, the determination of the taxes due, and the completion of the requisite forms. In recent years they have been supplemented by tax preparation services and software programs from TurboTax, H&R Block, and TaxAct among others.

Nevertheless, there are thousands of law firms and accounting firms of all sizes assisting businesses and individuals (including most law firms and many lawyers) in the preparation and filing of their tax returns. Putting this information on the Internet has helped some people better understand and deal with their taxes, but such information has not solved the problem for many taxpayers, and has been inadequate for the needs of many others. The need for professional consultation and advisory assistance remains high.

Indeed, Professor Susskind is expecting the creation of new functional categories of lawyer and nonlawyer jobs that will be designed to assist *practicing lawyers* in the use of the very internet and digital tools he apparently anticipates will be used effectively by *the general public*. New functional specialists like knowledge engineers and legal technologists can and will assist lawyers in providing their services more cost-effectively. However, for the reasons stated, the demand for one-to-one consultative advisory legal service will not be significantly reduced, much less replaced, anytime soon by packaged information services on the Internet.

I recently asked my own tax accountant, who is a partner in a prominent firm, what the impact of TurboTax, TaxAct and H&R Block had been on the nature and volume of his firm's tax work. His blunt answer surprised me: "Zero."

(5) THE MOVEMENT OF LEGAL WORK IN-HOUSE

Many of the legal services provided by law firms to businesses, governments and organizations in 1950 are now provided to such clients by their own law departments. Much of the routine and recurring work for organizations will continue to move in-house or to alternative legal service providers (who in turn will be supervised by the law departments for whom they work). In the process, a lot of the work of large and medium-sized organizations will continue to shift from traditional law firms to law departments, but the work will still be there to be done by lawyers inside rather than outside.

Many smaller and emerging organizations will not have a sufficient need for legal advice to justify the employment of a full-time lawyer, and larger clients cannot afford to have underutilized in-house lawyers awaiting a legal issue to address. Ergo there will be a continuing need for lawyers and law firms to support the work of law departments and to provide a range of legal services directly to other organizations and individuals in need of legal assistance.

(6) THE ROLE OF LEGAL KNOW-HOW AND RELATIONSHIPS

Familiarity with the legal process and with the personnel presiding over governmental legal operations and the courts is very important. Most of the know-how and relationships that lubricate the legal process are not accessible through books or on the Internet. Such know-how and relationships are the stock-in-trade of experienced lawyers, law firms and law departments.

(7) TECHNOLOGY

The two-edged sword of technology has increased the interaction of countries, cultures and economies, and has complicated the ways in which the world works. The manner in which many lawyers have used the capabilities provided by new technology has increased the complexity of documents and transactions. Technology is available to all sides and will be used by each side to their advantage, but it can't negotiate most agreements or resolve most disputes without human participation.

There is no reason to think that complexity will be conquered or decreased by computers. It is more likely that computers will continue to make the world a more complicated place. The recent manipulation of law firm internal records by criminals to divert client funds to fake accounts, and the emergence of "ransomware" attacks are two examples of the multifaceted impact of technology on legal services.

(8) HUMAN NATURE

There is a natural tendency for people to look for and believe in the aspects of a dispute or negotiation that are most favorable to themselves, and many are unwilling to accept the reality of the problems confronting them. Many are not as smart or as knowledgeable as they think they are. Clients benefit from the advice of disinterested experts who can help them evaluate the factual circumstances and the law relative to their situation and assist them in the implementation of their response.

Similar challenges exist for other professions. The tremendous increase in the amount of information about health care that is available on the Internet and in medical newsletters has enabled some people to attempt to diagnose and treat themselves for some maladies, but there remains a large unmet need for personal and knowledgeable medical services. People prefer to reach conclusions that they like rather than those they dislike. Efforts at self-diagnosis will help some, but many others would have been wiser to consult a doctor. The same is true for individuals and organizations with legal issues.

As a senior partner of a prominent Atlanta law firm was known to say, his favorite clients were wealthy individuals who died after writing their own wills.

CHAPTER SEVEN

The Future of the Legal Profession

Let me be clear—I believe that the legal profession will continue to experience significant changes in the future as it has over the last 70+ years. Most clients expect their own law departments, their outside law firms, and the ALSPs they use to find ways to reduce costs while improving the quality and functionality of the legal services they provide. Technology and the Internet, rather than replacing great numbers of lawyers or enabling many people to become their own lawyers, will enable lawyers, law firms and law departments to continue to expand and serve their markets more cost-effectively. Twenty-first century technology will assist all lawyers in keeping up with the burgeoning body of laws and regulations and their effect on our lives. Technology and the Internet may also enable the legal profession to serve on a profitable basis more of the currently underserved and unserved markets for legal services.

A number of recent trends will continue, including:

(1) THE MAGNITUDE AND COMPLEXITY OF THE LAW WILL CONTINUE TO INCREASE AND THE LEGAL SYSTEM WILL REQUIRE MORE LAWYER SUPPORT

There is no apparent end to the growing number of people on the face of the earth or to the complexity of our lives and commerce. As a result, new laws and regulations are an unavoidable fact of life that will continually create a need for additional analysis, interpretation, explanation and application. Many mature laws and regulations will need to be systematically pruned, and those that have become obsolete or unnecessarily burdensome will need to be changed or repealed. Technology will assist us with this process by helping us to cope with the increasing bulk and complexity of our laws and regulations, but it is unlikely that technology will significantly reduce the required number of lawyers.

(2) THE RANGE AND AMOUNT OF USEFUL LEGAL INFORMATION, KNOWLEDGE AND KNOW-HOW ACCESSIBLE ON THE INTERNET WILL CONTINUE TO INCREASE

There is a distinction between legal information and useful legal knowledge. Knowing the letter of the applicable law is only the beginning of the process of addressing a legal issue. Legal information does not become useful legal knowledge until it has been identified as relevant to specific legal issues, and has been thoughtfully analyzed and put to use in the process of solving problems, creating agreements or resolving disputes. Doing so requires legal education, training and experience.

Following World War II many firms began to build libraries of loose-leaf binders containing research memos and examples of documents and pleadings created in their practices in order to serve more efficiently and inexpensively the needs of their growing clientele, and law departments began to grow and do the same. In due course as computers facilitated the retention and organization of documents and research memoranda, the accumulated loose-leaf binders full of paper documents were relegated to the back-end of law libraries (those that still existed), and the related card catalogues were retired. Then electronic communications and the Internet made computer based and organized information and analysis readily available within and between law firms and law departments.

The need for every law firm and law department to create and maintain substantial knowledge management programs of their own has now been reduced by commercially available online systems. Law firms and law departments can access significantly increased amounts of legal information, knowledge and know-how using these systems—more quickly and more easily than at any time in the past. One important result has been to make law departments increasingly less dependent on private practice law firms for such information, knowledge, and know-how. All of the Elite Firms and most major firms maintain their own proprietary knowledge management systems that they augment with commercially available systems.

(3) TECHNOLOGY WILL CONTINUE TO AFFECT HOW LEGAL SERVICES ARE DELIVERED TO CLIENTS AND WHO DELIVERS THEM

As discussed in Chapter Two, the application of technology to the practice of law is having some of the same effects that technology has caused in other fields of endeavor. Technology has increased competition among legal service providers and is helping reduce the time required to deliver some legal services. Some of the economies realized from the application of new products and services are off-set by the added cost of the technology, and the training and personnel necessary to utilize it. Most new legal technology is accommodative rather than disruptive; it enables lawyers, law firms and law departments to improve their services and to provide them more quickly and cost-effectively.

The Internet and e-mail (presumably encrypted email to protect privileged and confidential information) have greatly facilitated communications between lawyers, their clients and others with whom they deal wherever they may be located, including those in other countries.

Technology and software companies offer hundreds of law practice management and law project management software tools to integrate law practice functions and facilitate the provision of legal services. Knowledge management tools provide access to much larger stores of legal information, knowledge and know-how. These tools are available to law departments as well as law firms and have reduced the reliance of law departments on private practice firms. The effects of technology on lawyers, law firms and law departments are significant and enduring, and will continue to drive changes in the legal profession for the foreseeable future.

(4) WE WILL SEE MORE DISAGGREGATION OF LEGAL PROJECTS INTO DISTINCT TASKS THAT WILL BE DISTRIBUTED AMONG APPROPRIATE SERVICE PROVIDERS

We are seeing an increase in the use of disaggregation as law departments seek the most cost-effective service providers to handle each segment of a legal transaction or dispute. In the past, when clients or law departments assigned projects to private practice firms they sent the entire project, which was then organized and staffed as the firms thought appropriate using their own personnel or subcontractors. The firms were able to realize high profit margins on relatively simple parts of these projects staffed by young associates, contract lawyers, paralegals and/or ALSPs. That era has largely ended.

Today clients with law departments often divide legal projects into discrete tasks based on the knowledge and skill required to address each of them, and then decide which provider should receive each assignment. They retain those tasks they can cost-effectively manage in-house, and select other legal service providers to handle the remainder based on the skills, prices and reliability of available suppliers. In doing so clients are taking increasing amounts of the low-hanging fruit from private practice law firms and doing the work themselves or assigning it to ALSPs. Document review activities are the largest and most obvious example.

Technology has facilitated disaggregation, but disaggregation has also increased complexity. Although each disaggregated service may be produced at a lower cost, clients will nonetheless have new management and supervision costs relating to the disaggregation, assignment, and reaggregation of the constituent parts properly and on a timely basis. Law departments will find it is necessary to supervise, coordinate and integrate such disaggregated projects with careful attention to results and cost in order to capture the economic benefits of the process.

(5) THE PERCENTAGE OF LEGAL WORK PERFORMED BY LAW DEPARTMENTS AND ALSPS WILL INCREASE AND THE PERCENTAGE PERFORMED BY PRIVATE PRACTICE FIRMS WILL DECREASE

In-house general counsel have established their ability and prerogative to manage the legal affairs of their employer-clients; they now rule the roost. Today's general counsel are under pressure to reduce costs while maintaining efficiency and quality.

Most large organizations have concluded that to the extent possible they need to control and manage inside of their organizations the legal aspects of their operations, both because of the importance of legal issues to the success of their enterprises and because of growing costs. To do so they are adding additional capability to their law departments and expect them to become more effective and efficient, and they are exhorting their general counsels to make less use of private practice firms (and when they do use them, to lower the costs of doing so).

As law departments become more self-confident and efficient, there is likely to be a reduction in the percentage of lawyers in private practice and an increase in the percentage in law departments. Such a shift will move some lawyers around on the playing field, but will not necessarily result in a reduction of the number of lawyers in the game.

As a general rule law departments cannot justify maintaining full-time experts in every subject they need to address. Consequently, there will continue to be many situations requiring private practice lawyers to assist clients in addressing issues of considerable importance that require expert assistance and in dealing with sporadic overloads.

Law departments are also making increased use of knowledge management programs and tools utilizing artificial intelligence. They are recruiting knowledge management lawyers and other personnel to assist with the process of accumulating and making available for retrieval the collective knowledge of the lawyers in their law department and the knowledge of their outside counsel. Such programs may require all of an organization's outside counsel to collaborate and make available to the client, and to the client's other outside counsel working on similar matters, their knowledge applicable to the issue at hand. The law department of DuPont has had such a program in place for many years.

Law departments are also encouraging standardization and programmability within their organizations. To the extent that a frequently recurring task or action can be standardized, the need for law department intervention is reduced, and nonlawyers can manage more of the tasks.

In-house lawyers will also continue to focus on supporting their employer-clients by avoiding legal disputes and facilitating their employer's capacity to grow their profitability. Some departments are also becoming income generators for their organizations by seeking opportunities to license underutilized company property or to identify legal claims against third parties and pursuing them on behalf of their employers. At least one law department of a major UK company (British Telecom) is utilizing an alternative business structure so that it can function like a law firm and sell some of its legal services to unrelated organizations.

Law departments also are learning to work differently, and will benefit from the utilization of some of the new job categories discussed in Chapter Nine, *New Opportunities for Lawyers and Legal Assistants.*

(6) LAW FIRMS, LAW DEPARTMENTS AND ALSPS WILL INCREASE THEIR UTILIZATION OF LESS EXPENSIVE LAWYERS AND LICENSED AND UNLICENSED SUPPORT PERSONNEL

The lawyer leverage used by many large and mid-sized law firms is likely to decline as more routine work is disaggregated and performed by law departments, or for law departments by ALSPs. Fees law firms would have received for this work will be peeled off by more efficient and less expensive service providers.

In recent years many corporate law departments have refused to pay for services provided by first year associates, and for some of the work of second year associates. They consider the newest associates to be apprentices learning their trade, and believe that the cost of their training should fall on their employers rather than on clients. This has had an adverse effect on the number of new associates employed by some law firms and on the profitability of some firms.

The income available to compensate many law firm partners will inevitably decline unless firms are able to replace some associates with lower cost lawyers or billable nonlawyer personnel and/or to raise the rates of their partners for consultative services enough to offset the declines in revenues resulting from the decline in leverage.

In response to these pressures law firms are employing more billable nonlawyer personnel and have been trying to raise the billing rates of their partners; they will continue to do so when they can. If leverage is reduced, the compensation of many partners, as in "the good old days," will increasingly be dependent on the income they are able to earn from their own work rather than from the services of others within their firms.

(7) MANY LAW FIRMS WILL BECOME MORE SPECIALIZED AND LESS LEVERAGED BECAUSE ROUTINE AND RECURRING WORK WILL BE TAKEN IN-HOUSE OR SERVICED BY ALSPs

As more routine and recurring work has moved in-house and to ALSPs, and as the American and world economies have grown (and with them the amount and complexity of law and regulation) many individual lawyers and law firms have responded by specializing in a relatively narrow range of legal issues and processes. Intensive specialization has become increasingly important and is commonplace in BigLaw firms today.

(8) THERE WILL BE MORE AND BETTER ALSPs PROVIDING SOME OF THE ROUTINE DOCUMENTS AND SERVICES THAT ARE PROVIDED BY LAW FIRMS

A variety of ALSPs are now competing with law firms to provide at a lower cost some of the services that are a part of the bundle of services that have traditionally been provided by law firms, and they are utilizing relatively inexpensive personnel, some who are lawyers and some who are not, to provide these services.

A few states are experimenting with a fundamental change in our legal system; the limited licensing of persons without law degrees to provide legal advice with respect to designated routine matters and documents without the supervision of a licensed attorney. (I refer to these limited license officers and technicians as "paralawyers" to distinguish them from the now ubiquitous "paralegals.") These developments are addressed more fully in Chapter Eight, *Alternative Legal Service Providers and Paralawyers.*

---

(9) SOLE PRACTITIONERS AND SMALL FIRMS WILL USE TECHNOLOGY, ALSPs AND PARALAWYERS TO PROVIDE LEGAL SERVICES AT MORE REASONABLE PRICES TO SOME EXISTING MARKETS FOR LEGAL SERVICES AS WELL AS TO THE UNDERSERVED AND UNSERVED MARKETS

Some sole practitioners and small firms are likely to team up with ALSPs and paralawyers to provide legal services to persons and organizations that cannot currently afford to pay the existing charges for legal services.

In the process of sorting out their role in the legal service arena some ALSPs/on-line form providers have concluded that they could improve their marketing, operations and profitability if they worked with, rather than against, practicing lawyers. As a result, in one way or another several of the online form companies and members of the bar are working together to offer consultation to clients. LegalZoom reports that they have "embraced lawyers and become quite adept with working with them" resulting in more than 200,000 one-on-one consultations between LegalZoom customers and licensed lawyers during the last five years. Rocket Lawyer is also connecting its customers with licensed lawyers. Some lawyers may find useful practice opportunities by participating in referral networks being created by consumer ALSPs like LegalZoom and Rocket Lawyer.

These organizations have found that they can increase the utility of their services and avoid attacks by the organized bar by integrating independent practicing lawyers into their service programs to answer client questions and to guide their use of their available forms. Consumer legal insurance providers, such as ARAG Group, have also created "in-network" provider networks.

Sole practitioners and small firms can also employ legal assistants and paralawyers to assist them in providing more economical legal services.

(10) LEGAL SERVICES WILL BE INCREASINGLY AVAILABLE TO THE PUBLIC IN SHOPPING CENTER AND BANK LOCATIONS STAFFED BY LAWYERS, LAW FIRMS, AND PARALAWYERS

A few year ago in Canada some law offices operated by Axess Law Professional Corporation were opened in a few Walmart stores. Axess currently has offices in 10 Walmart stores in Toronto and expects to have 18 offices in Walmart locations in Toronto and Ottawa by the end of 2016. Axess provides a wide range of legal services relating to wills, notary services, real estate transactions, powers of attorney, business law matters, and uncontested divorces. The firm has already prepared 25,000 wills (the usual price is $99), but does not undertake to represent any clients with complicated estate planning needs who they refer to other firms.

It did not take long for small law offices to appear in Walmarts in the United States. Kaine Law has opened offices in three Atlanta-area Walmart stores. The firm is primarily a personal injury and accident firm that retains only about 20 percent of the cases that originate in its offices and refers the remainder to other firms.

Another firm operating as "The Law Store" opened law offices in June of 2016 in two Walmart stores, one in Joplin and one in

Neosho, Missouri. It views itself as a full-service firm handling a wide variety of legal work including small business services, family law, traffic violations and misdemeanors, wills and powers of attorney, workers compensation claims and some personal injury work. All of its services are provided on a fixed fee basis. By the end of 2016 The Law Store anticipates opening two offices in Dallas Walmarts and three more in Missouri Walmarts. Both The Law Store and Kaine Law have websites to promote their services and that can be used to make appointments.

Walmart's Sam's Club division has teamed up with LegalZoom to provide its members with affordable legal help for their families and businesses. LegalZoom has developed a variety of legal solutions available to Sam's Club registered members on samsclub.com. The services include estate planning documents and a year of consultation about such documents with an independent attorney, as well as small business organization and intellectual property protection. Club members will also save up to 25 percent on all other LegalZoom documents including LLCs, corporations, trademarks, and more.

Shopping mall developers and retailers other than Walmart may see the advantage of providing space for legal service outlets in their facilities. I would not be surprised if some banks began to follow the Walmart example by leasing excess branch bank space to one or more law firms.

(11) THERE WILL BE CHANGES IN DISPUTE RESOLUTION

Chapter Ten is devoted to this subject and addresses a variety of issues including changes in discovery and legal process rules, specialized courts, proactive judges, early neutral evaluation, better utilization of the common law and precedent, restructuring judicial responsibilities, virtual courts, and non-judicial dispute resolution including mediation, arbitration, and new types of settlement services.

(12) COMPETITION WILL CONTINUE TO PUT DOWNWARD PRESSURE ON LEGAL FEES THAT WILL RESTRAIN LAW FIRM PROFITABILITY EXCEPT FOR THE ELITE FIRMS AND THEIR ILK

This subject has been discussed at length in my 2012 book, *Declining Prospects*. Suffice it to say here that even with declining law school enrollments American law schools have continued to overproduce law school graduates for a number of years and may still be doing so. The excess supply combined with technological advancements and ALSPs will exert a constant downward pressure on law firm profitability except possibly for the leading firms at the top of the legal service industry.

(13) EXPECT A REAPPRAISAL OF THE LATERAL MOVEMENT OF LAWYERS TAKING CLIENTS WITH THEM TO OTHER LAW FIRMS, AND INCREASED EFFORTS TO RESTRAIN SUCH ACTIVITY

The key issue is whether the relocating lawyer has solicited, directly or indirectly, the representation of one or more of his firm's clients prior to the termination of his relationship with his current firm. Despite the clear agency law prohibition against an agent's solicitation of the business of their principals' clients while still working for them, the ABA's Model Rule 5.6 has been viewed by some as sanctioning lawyers to solicit the work of their current firms' clients before they depart to another firm or to set up their own.

Rule 5.6 provides:

"A lawyer shall not participate in offering or making:

(a) a partnership, shareholder, operating, employment, or other similar type of agreement that restricts the right of a lawyer to practice *after termination of the relationship* (emphasis supplied), except an agreement concerning benefits upon retirement; or

(b) An agreement in which a restriction on the lawyer's right to practice is part of the settlement of a client controversy."

Note that 5.6(a) relates to agreements that restrict a lawyer's actions "after termination of the relationship." Note also that the rule deals with "agreement" between lawyers and their firms, and is silent on agency law restrictions. It does not grant to lawyer-agents the right to solicit their firm's client base while still an agent.

Unlike unfinished business claims, the amount of damages for breach of loyalty claims is unrelated to the solvency or insolvency of the lawyer's current firm; the amount of potential damages may not be dependent on a proof of actual damages, and punitive damages may be available. Consequently, as firms become more aggressive about protecting their relationships under agency law, it is likely to become harder and riskier for dissatisfied lawyers to move to other firms, and for other firms to evaluate the ability of a proposed lateral entry lawyer to move "his or her clients" to them. If the acquiring firms play an active role in the violation of a lawyer's duty of loyalty, they may also be exposed to liability.

Many lawyers, judges and bar associations appear to have confused the right of clients to select their lawyers, with a right of lawyers to appropriate their firms' assets with impunity while still members or employees of their firms. The fundamental duty of loyalty of agents to their principals is still the law of the land. *After termination of the relationship*, Model Rule 5.6 protects the moving lawyer's right to seek the representation of his former firm's clients, but not before.

Why does this matter? Often firms bring in partners/counsel from other firms in anticipation that they will bring with them new clientele. Without such an assurance, the new firm may be less likely to commit to a prospective new lawyer or his or her compensation arrangement, and the prospective new lawyer is less likely to terminate his or her existing relationship without assurance as to his or her compensation arrangements. As a result, there is often a conversation and sometimes an agreement about the new business that the relocating lawyer will produce.

Many major firms have been destabilized by lawyer *free agency*. When a partner leaves a firm and is able to take important clients with him to his new firm, not only has his former firm lost important clients, but other partners in his former firm are more likely to consider their options as well. Once a lawyer leaves a firm for more compensation from another, he or she is more likely to move again in response to the prospect of further increased income.

Numerous firms are now seeking to protect themselves from partners leaving with "firm" clients by building into their partnership agreements terms that are designed to satisfy some courts' application of Rule 5.6 while inflicting financial penalties for unwanted departures. Such provisions include delayed returns of capital, and compensation arrangements calling for refunds or forfeitures of some compensation as well as bonus claw-backs tied to length of tenure and possibly the volume of business achieved. A relocating partner may forfeit a bonus from his new firm if he does not remain with it for a stated period of time, or if he fails to produce a stated amount of new business.

I also suspect that partners in the Elite Firms as well as those in other firms that provide unfunded retirement benefits might not qualify for such benefits if they left their firm prior to retirement and continued to practice law with a competitor whether or not they took some firm clients with them.

---

(14) OTHER DEVELOPMENTS

In addition to the changes already noted, "New Model" law firms are also growing in importance in the USA. They take several different forms including virtual firms that are usually loose confederations of lawyers operating from home offices. Other new model firms like Taylor English Duma LLP in Atlanta have a more traditional method of working while employing less leverage, occupying less expensive offices, and charging lower rates than their major firm competitors for similar services. Chapter Fifteen of *Declining Prospects* addressed the New Model law firms in greater detail.

The developments anticipated in this chapter will have little effect on the Elite Firms as long as they are able to maintain their professional strengths. However, the lower echelon of BigLaw firms are likely to experience a further reduction in the amount of routine work they receive. They will increase their efforts to obtain legal work requiring higher levels of skill and experience as they try to maintain or raise their charges for such services. Doing so is much easier said than done.

Others firms will stress their cost-effective services for smaller organizations that cannot afford to maintain full-service law departments. Some brave law practice entrepreneurs may even try to become sufficiently efficient (or their lawyers may be willing to accept lower levels of compensation) so that they can provide a cost-effective alternative to some small contemporary in-house law departments. And some firms will focus on the underserved or unserved lower end of the market and find better and less expensive ways to profitably provide legal services in those markets.

CHAPTER EIGHT

Alternative Legal Service Providers and Paralawyers

ALSPs

The services being provided by various ALSPs include legal process outsourcing (document review in litigation and due diligence work in business transactions), contract management, regulatory compliance, forms, customizable document libraries, document drafting services, legal research, routine seasonal or unpredictable legal work in some practice areas, and online dispute resolution platforms.

The most controversial of these ALSPs are those that offer their services directly to the consuming public rather than to law firms and law departments. They are much more likely to be challenged by the organized bar and run afoul of prohibitions on the unauthorized practice of law. As a practical matter lawyers (sole practitioners, law firms and law departments) can use the services of individuals or organizations that are not licensed to practice law in any way they want as long as they maintain the relationship with their client, assume responsibility for the work, and endorse it as their own; that's how law firms and law departments have been using legal assistants for decades.

Many ALSPs use some law school graduates to provide their services. They are often able to employ lawyers at compensation substantially below the levels paid by major law firms because of the current excess supply of law school graduates.

One early-entrant ALSP, LegalZoom, currently offers its services directly to the consuming public in all 50 states. It is an online interactive purveyor of self-help legal documents. It initially dealt directly with the *clients* that used its services in the place of an attorney, and it was accused of the *unauthorized practice of law* by multiple state bar associations.

It has survived these challenges including recent cases in the South Carolina and the North Carolina Courts. The South Carolina Supreme Court concluded that virtually all of the South Carolina forms available on LegalZoom "are available online to South Carolina citizens via other self-help portals at websites maintained by various South Carolina governmental agencies." The referee also concluded that the documents available on LegalZoom did not provide legal advice and the company did not assist customers in creating documents or filling them out.

LegalZoom settled its litigation with The North Carolina Bar Association by agreeing to support legislation that would exclude websites offering automated document preparation from the definition of the "practice of law" if consumers were offered specified protections. Such statutory protections were recently enacted by the North Carolina Legislature. They provide for (1) the review and approval of the available templates by a North Carolina lawyer, (2) notice to consumers that the forms aren't a substitute for consulting a lawyer, (3) consumer retention of the right to sue the provider in the

North Carolina courts, and (4) the unlimited right of consumers to recover damages for breaches of representations and warranties.

LegalZoom has also recently established operations in England and Wales in association with Quality Solicitors, a network of independent firms of solicitors that operate under the Quality Solicitors franchise and trade name. Because of the relatively narrow definition of Reserved Legal Services in England and Wales, LegalZoom is able to provide a greater range of services to consumers there than in the United States. It would not be surprising for the company to use this less restrictive legal services environment to experiment with the expansion and improvement of its legal services offerings elsewhere.

ALSPs that provide support to law firms and law departments as opposed to individual clients are much less subject to unauthorized practice complaints.

Novus Law, a New York based company with more than a dozen offices worldwide and over 1,200 employees, is an example of a legal process outsourcer involved in using its employees (many of whom are attorneys) to review, manage, analyze and organize documents for large scale litigation and corporate transactions, primarily for law departments. In addition it examines, organizes and analyzes clients' documents and other case-related materials, and prepares motions, briefs and discovery responses. It also provides professional management services to assist law departments and law firms with the management of engagements and portfolios of engagements. Consequently, it is not engaged in the practice of law; it is supplying support services to lawyers.

Axiom Global, Inc., a C corporation for tax purposes, is not a law firm either. It started as a long-term legal temp placement agency, but in 2010 it created a new legal outsourcing or "managed services" division. This division provides routine and semi-routine services (like document review, and recurring contract negotiation) which are often seasonal in nature and would not justify the employment by a law department of another full-time lawyer.

Axiom recently entered into a multi-layered three-year partnership to handle British Telecom's commercial contract work, and provides technology that helps BT's in-house lawyers track and accelerate workflow and improve the allocation of their resources. Business units are able to deal directly with Axiom, enabling the law department to focus on more important work.

Because Axiom is not a law firm it can have nonlawyer investors and raise capital from venture capitalists and other private investors. It can also supply law departments with nonlawyer drafters and negotiators. However, it and its lawyer-employees cannot give legal opinions, or represent clients in court, which limits the range of legal work it can provide through its attorneys and its nonlawyer staff.

Entities like Axiom are also supplying lawyers to law firms and law departments on a temporary or short-term basis. Some English law firms have set up and are operating affiliates that do the same thing, and some American firms may follow suit.

Another form of ALSP that received a lot of attention in the legal press a couple of years ago was Clearspire, a Washington, D.C. based organization composed of a law firm and a separate but related business entity that managed the business operations and support services of the law firm. The business arm was paid by the law firm for providing such services.

The concept received enthusiastic attention from the legal media. The arrangement permitted nonlawyer investment and revenue-sharing in the business arm, while the Clearspire law firm provided traditional legal services. The law firm announced that starting in 2014 it expected to add 50 to 100 experienced lawyers from major firms each year for five years, but before the year was out the law firm part of the enterprise closed, apparently because of insufficient revenue to support its operations.

There is a growing number of ALSPs of various types as well as of consulting firms assisting law firms and law departments in the management and production of their work. Because of the increasing economic burden of legal services we can expect to see more and different types of ALSPs in the years ahead.

PARALAWYERS

Louisiana law, which is based on civil law rather than on the English common law, has long provided for a class of legal service providers who are not required to be lawyers; notaries public who are authorized to prepare legal documents for routine matters such as wills, trusts, marriage contracts, corporate organizations, mortgages, real estate sales, powers of attorney, contracts, etc.

Notaries are not allowed to give "legal" advice or to appear in court for a fee on behalf of clients, but they are allowed to explain or recommend documents necessary to effect some legal transactions or relationships. They are also authorized to prepare documents including inventories, appraisals, wills, matrimonial contracts, conveyances, and most other contracts in writing. Lawyers licensed in Louisiana automatically possess all of the powers of notaries, but notaries are limited in the services they can provide and must pass examination and be licensed before providing any of them.

The Supreme Court of the State of Washington commissioned a study in 2003 which found that the legal needs of the consuming public in Washington were not being met. In 2012, after nine years of deliberation, the Court responded by adopting rules that have established two boards to create the framework for the licensing and regulation of persons who are not members of the bar to provide legal advice with respect to certain legal matters that are currently viewed to involve the practice of law.

In creating the boards the Court exercised its exclusive power to regulate and oversee the practice of law in the State of Washington. The Court was motivated by the unregulated activities of many untrained, unsupervised *nonlawyer practitioners* who daily did harm to clients in the state, and its desire to enable the public to obtain high quality civil legal services provided by qualified individuals at an affordable price.

The boards are permitted to license individuals to advise and assist clients in a few approved legal practice areas. Such persons will have to meet specified educational and training requirements, pass examinations, and periodically update their knowledge in order to serve as *Limited License Legal Technicians* or as *Limited Practice Officers*.

The first area of practice designated for Limited License Legal Technicians is Domestic Relations. They cannot represent clients in court, they cannot negotiate on behalf of a client, and they can only prepare legal documents that have been approved by the Limited License Legal Technician Board. Applications for the licensing exam were accepted in March of 2015, and fifteen or more persons have qualified and been licensed in this area.

The Limited Practice Board of the Washington State Bar is authorized to regulate Limited Practice Officers who may be licensed to select, prepare, and complete legal forms that the Board has approved in connection with the closing of loans, extensions of credit, and sales or other transfers of real or personal property. One hundred and ninety-two persons had passed the required qualification exam as of October 2016.

There is a continuing controversy about the nature, scope and operations of these boards. It remains to be seen how this experiment will play out.

In 1998 California created a category of compensated *Legal Document Assistants* (LDAs) who are not lawyers but who are authorized to assist members of the public representing themselves in legal matters including assistance with the preparation of legal documents. LDAs are experts at form preparation and procedure and can help with many different areas, such as divorce, wills, deeds, guardianships, and many more. California has also authorized nonlawyer advisors designated *Unlawful Detainer Assistants* and *Immigration Consultants*.

Paralawyers add a new category to the ranks of legal service providers and represent the opening wedge of what could be a significant expansion of the class of nonlawyers authorized to provide limited legal services. The creation of these new categories of licensed providers recognizes that many members of the public have been priced out of the legal advice market and that persons providing a specific limited legal service do not need to know everything that law students learn in a three year JD program.

The supreme courts of most states have the power to regulate and control the practice of law within the borders of their state. As a result, the supreme courts, rather than state bar associations, have the power to determine who can provide legal services in their states and what standards have to be met.

This power was recently reinforced by a decision of the U.S. Supreme Court (*North Carolina Board of Dental Examiners v. Federal Trade Commission*) dealing with dental boards. The decision concluded that the North Carolina Board of Dental Examiners could not regulate the dental profession in the state unless the board itself was actively supervised by the state. Presumably, the same test would apply to state bar associations and would require their supervision directly by an agency of the state which would normally be the state's supreme court unless another state agency has been created for that purpose or assigned the responsibility.

Other state supreme courts may decide to expand the range of legal service providers in order to fill the need for legal assistance for citizens who cannot otherwise afford the services of a licensed member of the bar.

CHAPTER NINE

New Opportunities for Lawyers and Legal Assistants

A lthough Professor Susskind is pessimistic about the future need for lawyers, or at least the need for anything like the number of lawyers we currently have, he allays some of his pessimism by predicting "a promising range of new opportunities and new careers for people trained in the law." I agree that there will be a growing need for new types of jobs in the legal profession and new employees. And he believes, and I agree, that there will be a growing demand for lawyers with one or more functional skills that in the past were not recognized as categories of law practice skills.

FUNCTIONAL SPECIALISTS

I think we will see new ways of slicing and dicing the work customarily done by lawyers, large firms and law departments that were mostly unknown in the past. As a result, there will be new types of legal service jobs for some lawyers in law firms and law departments, as well as for some other professionals.

After the end of World War II many large law firms and law departments began to use nonlawyer administrators and personnel to assist with the non-legal aspects of their administration such as accounting, billing and collections, facilities, finance, personnel management, record keeping and supplies. Recently law departments have realized the advantages of using the services of specialists they share within their organization who are not lawyers to facilitate the operation of their legal function.

This broader view of law firm and law department operations and management involves the active participation of both lawyer and nonlawyer professionals in the legal services production and delivery process ("operations") rather than the nonlawyers merely supporting lawyers ("administration"). As a result, there will be new types of legal service jobs for some lawyers in law firms and law departments, as well as for other professionals.

These jobs will be focused on the functions involved in performing legal work such as coordinating activities, document assembly, managing relationships, managing research, pricing, utilizing personnel and technology, etc. These functional technicians will find new ways to organize the work and to assist with the production and management of legal projects.

The categories of such functional legal jobs are likely to include some of the following: business process analysts and advisors, knowledge managers, librarians, management consultants, operations managers, practice group administrators, pricing specialists, project and dispute resolution coordinators, project managers, research specialists, risk managers, and technologists.

Large law firms and law departments are more likely to use fulltime functional specialists, with smaller firms and law departments using fewer of them, and obtaining some such assistance from law practice consulting firms and ALSPs. Law graduates with an interest in the business and operational sides of law firm and law department operations may elect to forego a career as a practicing lawyer and focus instead on law firm or law department management and operations. For this reason dual JD/MBA programs may grow in popularity. It remains to be seen if and how clients might agree to pay for such support services.

PRICING SPECIALISTS

During the *Raise the Bar* initiative sponsored by the ABA's Section of Litigation in 2005-06 one participant suggested that some companies might turn over the purchase of their legal services to their procurement departments; most of the other participants thought such a development to be highly improbable.

Nonetheless, ten years later in early 2015, I attended a seminar sponsored by *Buying Legal Counsel* that explored how law departments and procurement personnel from major companies could obtain the best value and price for the legal services they purchase from law firms and alternative legal service providers. Many of the presenters and participants were corporate procurement professionals, some of whom were trained as lawyers and some not, including folks with titles such as Senior Vice President Professional Services Sourcing; Director of Global Procurement; Strategic Sourcing Manager; and Manager—Strategic Sourcing—Legal & Professional Services, who were officers of companies like Boston Scientific, Bristol-Myers Squibb, Citigroup, and Intel.

An increasing number of law departments and law firms employ specialists to assist with the analysis, structuring and pricing of legal service proposals, and to conduct requests for proposals and auctions. Lawyers (and nonlawyer professionals) who are specialists in pricing legal services and negotiating fee arrangements are in demand.

TRAINERS

As partners have devoted more of their time to wooing and servicing clients they have had less time to train their younger colleagues, and thus far most law schools have been ill-equipped to provide such training. As a result some firms and departments employ lawyers as training specialists working as coaches to provide the training young lawyers and staff rarely receive from busy partners. These professionals may also train other company or firm personnel so they can better understand and manage the legal issues and problems that are involved in their work.

ONLINE DISPUTE RESOLUTION

Some new job categories are developing in connection with litigation and nontraditional dispute resolution such as online dispute resolution specialists, and will be addressed in Chapter Ten when we consider reforms in dispute resolution systems.

It remains unclear how many of these new types of lawyer jobs will be created and how many may not be lawyer-preferred positions.

WHERE WILL THE NEW JOBS BE?

Many of the new jobs will develop in larger law firms, law departments, and ALSPs. It is also likely that a variety of nontraditional employers, some of which have been employing lawyers for a long time and some that are relatively new, will provide growing employment opportunities for lawyers. Some of these jobs have existed on a small scale for many years, but they are likely to increase in number and sophistication in the years ahead.

Other than law firms and law departments, what sort of organizations will these employers be? Some of the big international accounting firms (and their affiliates) started providing a limited range of legal services in the United States prior to the Enron debacle and cut back afterwards, but have continued to provide legal services in other countries. It would be surprising if they do not re-enter the legal market in the United States. There are a variety of services they or their affiliates might provide including some services now being provided by ALSPs. They might also re-enter some aspects of the legal advisory market even though they would not, under current rules, be able to provide legal opinions or appear in court for clients.

The major legal publishers that already employ many lawyers will be hiring more as they expand their services in print and over the Internet. A few are also providing legal advisory services, and some have also expanded into legal technology and knowledge engineering. Some are also merging with know-how providers and will need additional trained lawyers to support these services.

Many alternative legal service providers and legal process outsourcers like Novas Law employ some law school graduates to help provide their services. These ALSPs and outsourcers are seeking to expand the services they offer and can be expected to employ more lawyers to do so.

Some lawyers may find useful practice opportunities by participating in referral networks being created by consumer ALSPs like LegalZoom and Rocket Lawyer. These organizations have found that they can increase the utility of their services and avoid attacks by the organized bar by integrating independent members of the bar into their service programs to answer user questions and to guide their use of the available forms.

Other ALSPs employ lawyers that they in turn lease temporarily, or provide on a contract basis, to law departments and law firms.

Traditional consulting firms and some dedicated legal consulting practices are employing more lawyers to assist in providing advice with respect to legal process analysis, legal project management, legal risk management, and the operation of law departments.

CHAPTER TEN

Dispute Resolution and Other Reforms

Litigation and other forms of dispute resolution are the largest part of the annual cost to clients for legal services in the United States. There is also a significant cost to the public of maintaining our local, state and federal judicial systems. E-discovery services alone are forecast to cost annually in excess of $14 billion by 2020. The cost-ineffectiveness and limited accessibility of our existing judicial system are apparent. Consequently, any serious plan to increase the cost-effectiveness of the legal services systems in the United States must provide a better and more economical way to resolve most disputes.

There are several possible approaches to reducing the cost of disputes that could be implemented within the existing judicial systems, including changes in discovery and in other legal process rules; increased use of electronic records, documents and communications; increased use of online conferencing; more specialized courts; reforming the judicial management of litigation; and better use of our common law system and resources.

Private dispute resolution procedures and services may also play a role in improving the dispute resolution process and reducing its costs.

It's estimated that more than 90% of all claims filed in courts in the USA are settled before trial. This startling percentage suggests that the costs, delays and uncertainties inherent in the use of existing public judicial systems are unacceptably high for most users; however, the high rate of settlement may also be a result of the parties obtaining a better understanding of the strengths and weaknesses of their positions from extensive discovery. Nevertheless, comparisons of the costs of judicial proceedings in the United States to those in other countries tell us that our costs are significantly higher. We need to find better and less expensive ways to resolve disputes.

CHANGES IN DISCOVERY AND LEGAL PROCESS RULES

Discovery is estimated to constitute between 50% and 80% of the cost of civil litigation in the United States. Changes in the Federal Rules of Civil Procedure that may curtail discovery costs and shorten the duration of civil cases were recently approved by the Judicial Conference and the U.S. Supreme Court, and became effective on December 1, 2015. One of the important changes is a requirement that the discovery sought be "proportional to the needs of the case." Although there are differing views of the likely impact of the new rules, many commentators expect they will reduce the cost of civil litigation in the Federal courts, and, if the past is prologue, many states will follow suit.

Other proposals to address the excessive costs of discovery include the adoption of the English rule that requires the losing party to pay the winning party's reasonable attorneys' fees which would include the winner's costs of discovery.

INCREASED USE OF ELECTRONIC RECORDS, DOCUMENTS AND COMMUNICATIONS

Considerable progress has been made in some courts with the use of electronic filings and documents which can expedite recovery of relevant documents and information and the time and money required to file and recover relevant documents. The ability of judges to conduct hearings about procedural and other matters electronically substantially reduces the time required of the parties and their counsel by eliminating travel to and waiting time at the court house.

SPECIALIZED COURTS

We are beginning to realize that it is impractical to expect judges to be Masters of the Universe responsible for the application of the entire body of law on every subject in their jurisdictions. Georgia has a specialized tax court where cases dealing with state taxation are tried by a judge with deep experience in the tax laws and regulations of the state. North Carolina has long had a highly regarded business court, and Georgia has recently created a business court in the county that includes most of the City of Atlanta. Most states have long had specialized criminal courts and juvenile courts. Delaware has its Chancery Court for the resolution of disputes involving the internal affairs of Delaware corporations and other forms of business entities. Our legal system would benefit by having more specialized courts.

JUDICIAL CASE MANAGEMENT AND EARLY NEUTRAL EVALUATION

The Civil Procedure Rules adopted in the courts of England and Wales in 1999 made judges responsible for the management of their cases rather than permitting the parties to control the pace and shape of the litigation. In effect the judges became active participants in the matters before them rather than serving as neutral umpires.

The purpose of judicial case management is to provide a fair environment for the resolution of disputes enabling the parties to prepare for settlement or trial while resolving individual issues as early as possible. The parties are required to cooperate in the process, and emphasis is placed on mediation and early resolution. The court takes active management of the dispute and determines the matters to be addressed, as well as how much and what sort of discovery is appropriate at each stage of the proceedings. This latter requirement goes beyond the "proportionality test" established in the new U.S. Federal discovery rules adopted last year.

Judges trained in case management and mediation would actively manage the proceedings before them encouraging the parties to develop their factual information and resolve their dispute while controlling the timetable and scheduling a substantive case management conference if the dispute has not already been resolved. By taking control of the proceedings the case-management judge helps eliminate inequalities between the parties with respect to information or resources while encouraging the parties to reach a just settlement of their dispute. Among the issues to be considered by the judge are the relationship between cost and benefit of proposed actions, the best way to promote a prompt resolution of the dispute, and the proportionality of the actions taken to the amount at issue in the dispute.

Over the past several decades, many changes to the Federal Rules of Civil Procedure have been intended to encourage and require more active case management, particularly in discovery and early case planning. The 2015 changes to the Federal Rules of Civil Procedure include new case management requirements designed to encourage a just, speedy and less expensive resolution of the proceeding. The state courts need to pursue similar efforts to encourage and support active case management.

Additional information about what has been going on in England and Wales can be found in Judge John Toulmin's 2012 book, *Expanding the Horizons.* Judge Toulmin served for 15 years as a judge of the Official Referees' Court (subsequently re-named the Technology and Construction Court) of the High Court of England and Wales, and was one of the most esteemed barristers and judges in the United Kingdom and the European Community. He served as President of the European Bar Association (the CCBC), and for more than 13 years as Chairman of the Board of Trustees of the European Law Academy in Trier, Germany prior to his untimely death in 2012.

Judge Toulmin believed that dispute resolution was a continuum beginning with mediation and ending, if necessary, with a trial, accompanied by the judge's active participation in the process until a resolution had been reached. He proposed, and practiced in his court, active judicial involvement from day one in each case as he set both the parameters for the case and its presentation, and actively shared his views of the case and its prospects from an early stage with the lawyers and their clients on both sides of the dispute. What Judge Toulmin proposed, and what is being done in some courts, can be achieved to a significant extent within our existing legal system.

Some sort of specialized professional training of judges in active judicial case management would likely be desirable if we were to utilize the principals of active case management in our courts.

THE BULK OF THE COMMON LAW

The growing bulk of the common law and the way it is used by many lawyers and judges continues to burden the judicial process. The historic complexity of our 50 state legal systems with an overlay of the federal system is a significant contributor to the costs (time and money) of resolving disputes in the United States. Approximately 33,000 judges preside over trial-level courts; there are approximately 12,000 state court judges with general jurisdiction, and an additional 18,000 state judges of limited jurisdiction as well as about 670 federal district court judges and over 350 federal bankruptcy judges. These are the frontline judges who hear arguments, take evidence, and either instruct the jury in the law or decide the case themselves. Their work is often supplemented and supported by magistrate judges and special masters appointed by the district courts.

The decisions of these trial judges are generally subject to review and possible reversal by appellate courts or courts of appeal. The federal government and most states have two levels of appellate courts; an intermediate court of appeals and a supreme court. Most of the appellate courts' opinions are available to the public and the legal profession through printed or electronic publishing systems. Also available are the reports of the U.S. Tax Court, the Court of International Trade, the 94 U. S. District Courts, U.S. Bankruptcy Courts, various other special courts, and a significant number of administrative boards and commissions.

The number of legal opinions seems to be increasing exponentially and the number of volumes of federal and state opinions continue to increase every year. The U.S. Supreme Court produces 80 to 90 opinions a year. There is considerable confusion about the various types of decisions issued by the U.S. Circuit Courts of Appeal and which of their decisions are "binding precedent." Although the Circuit Courts of Appeal disposed of 56,381 cases "on the merits" in 2004, over 80% did not result in a published opinion. There is an ongoing discussion in and out of the courts and academia as to the "binding precedential value" of the "unpublished opinions," some of which are published in the West's Federal Appendix or elsewhere.

In addition to the federal appellate court opinions, there are the opinions of federal trial courts and of the state appellate courts, and the regulations and decisions of federal and state administrative agencies. As a result it is difficult for many lawyers to keep up with the law relevant to their practice. Computers, and Internet based knowledge management programs have helped.

The more possibly relevant cases and administrative decisions that are found, the more work there is to be done, especially by lawyers who are not specialists. It is increasingly difficult for any lawyer to maintain a high level of familiarity with many different areas of practice. Specialists have the advantage of focusing their practices on a relatively narrow area of the law in a limited number of jurisdictions which reduces the number of opinions and administrative rulings that a specialist must master in order to maintain his or her expertise.

The growing burden of our case law has been evident for more than a century and grows more evident each year. As far back as 1906, Roscoe Pound, the Dean of the Harvard Law School and one of the great legal scholars and commentators of the twentieth century, criticized the common law system. He expressed concern that "the defects inherent in our system of case law were obvious as a result of its lack of certainty, confusion, incompleteness, and the waste of labor entailed by its prodigious bulk." The prodigious bulk of case law that concerned Dean Pound 110 years ago is vastly bulkier in today's large digital world.

Although computers and the Internet enable lawyers to access all of these materials more rapidly and completely than in the past, once found, the possibly relevant material must be examined and digested in order to determine its relevance to the situation at hand, and to explain and utilize it. The issue with computers is not that they are eliminating the need for lawyers; it is that without computers the common law would become entirely unmanageable.

HOW SOME LAWYERS MISUSE THE COMMON LAW

Another significant factor contributing to the excessive cost of our legal system is the way in which our prodigious bulk of case law is sometimes used by lawyers with the acquiescence of the judiciary. Frequently, the lawyers on both sides of a case will research the opinions of all of the states and the opinions of all of the federal courts for "authority." Some may also examine legal decisions in other countries. They will cite in their briefs any decision in their jurisdiction that they think may provide some support to their position, and may cite as well any other state or federal decisions that they believe can be viewed as supporting their view of some aspect of the issue or issues under consideration and helpful to their case, even though none of these extraterritorial decisions constitute binding legal precedent.

After they have conducted all of this research, they want to use it, so the briefs and memoranda they prepare are often excessive in size, complexity, and expense. The extra cost involved in researching and briefing the appellate court decisions in all fifty states and the decisions of the federal courts is often an inappropriate and unnecessary cost burden on clients.

In many cases, of course, neither the parties nor the lawyers have the resources to conduct and brief such extensive research. But highly motivated and well-funded parties can hire highly motivated and well-funded lawyers, and the temptation and incentive for lawyers to go overboard can become irresistible. Judges need not tolerate bloated and extraneous briefing, and there is room for significant cost savings through enhanced judicial management of runaway litigants.

Indeed, much litigation practice could be streamlined if proceeding focused more narrowly on the questions: "Is there a controlling precedent in this jurisdiction?" and then "Are there any analogous decisions in this jurisdiction?" There was a time, even in the most complex and high stakes case, when a one page brief citing the controlling precedent was all that was required to make a case or to resolve an appeal. Such a simple and bold presentation would be extremely unlikely today in similar cases.

The judge hearing a case is not bound to follow the law in another jurisdiction. The only relevance of a case in another jurisdiction is as a possibly thoughtful analysis of similar facts and the legal issue at hand.

In a situation without a binding precedent the judge is free to reach whatever reasonable conclusion he or she thinks appropriate without regard for the conclusions reached in other jurisdictions. In the present environment, however, some lawyers appear to be obsessed with citing authority from a nonbinding opinion in another state rather than stating a reasoned argument, and the more cases cited, from whatever source, the better.

Of course, counsel may like the outcome of a case in another jurisdiction involving a similar issue, and may elect to recommend the same solution to the court. And for a matter of first impression in a particular jurisdiction, a court will often find it helpful to explore the experience and decisions of courts in other states on similar issues. In the absence of a binding precedent, a Judge facing an unsettled issue in his jurisdiction for the first time can take guidance from those who have faced the same issue elsewhere. But justice and judicial economy are not automatically well-served when counsel cite each and every decision from every conceivable jurisdiction on the most remotely related points. Judges can and should demand focused, informative briefing from counsel, and should not tolerate the submission of unnecessarily bloated and irrelevant material.

The role of judges is to judge. They can reach the same decision as another judge in another jurisdiction, but such a decision is necessarily their own. It is a reflection of the judge's own best view of the meaning of the law and precedent in the judge's jurisdiction.

Unfortunately, the burden on the courts is sometimes increased as a result of some lawyers quoting words or phrases out of context or otherwise manipulating cited material that appears to support a conclusion which is in fact irrelevant or inconsistent with a fair reading of the cited case. Consequently, opposing counsel and judges (and their clerks) cannot rely on the briefs before them. They must read each case that has been relied upon to be certain that the holding has been properly stated and applied.

The courts are partially responsible for this breakdown in legal craftsmanship, because they have the power to require that lawyers use the system properly. A part of the breakdown is also attributable to the growing burden of the common law on the judges themselves, their increasing caseloads, and their necessary reliance on judicial clerks to assist them in the processing of their decisions.

While growth in the number of lawsuits has accelerated, Congress and state assemblies have failed to increase the size of their judiciaries proportionately. Consequently, many courts are being overwhelmed as the population grows. In addition, many cases today are much larger and more complicated than cases in the past, increasing the burden on the courts even more than the growing number of cases would indicate.

The single biggest problem with the judicial systems of the United States and many of the individual states today is overloaded courts and judges that are the result of the failure of governments to adequately fund their court systems. Overloads have led to extended delays in the processing of cases as the parties wait months for decisions on routine motions, and to mistakes by judges due to their inability to devote adequate time and attention to the many issues and cases before them. Their overloads make it impossible for judges to engage in effective case management. Highly motivated parties, and well-funded counsel will fill the space resulting from delays with more and more arguments and issues.

The proliferation of litigation is in part attributable to a third trend; the creation of legal causes of action by legislators as solutions to political and societal problems. The ability to create new statutory schemes for litigants to seek justice for various "wrongs" has been of tremendous value to politicians, who view such solutions as pleasing to constituents, easy, and cheap. Rarely does a legislature pledge additional resources to the court system to help it deal with the adjudication of a new class of claims. When citizens exercise their newly minted rights and place additional burdens on the judicial system, lawyers are often blamed rather than the politicians who created the new rights without adequately funding the courts responsible for dealing with them. The creation of these new rights has also been very profitable for some lawyers and their firms.

What is perfectly clear is that the cost of sorting through and dealing with vast quantities of legal material adds significantly to the cost of the legal process. Computerized legal research has increased the speed with which lawyers can identify cases that appear to be relevant to the subject of their concerns, and computers may be more thorough in what they find. Nonetheless, once the cases have been found, the lawyers and the judge (or his or her clerks) are still faced with reading and analyzing them, and the judge must reach and document an opinion.

NONJUDICIAL DISPUTE RESOLUTION

There is a growing number of alternative dispute resolution procedures and systems, ranging from the well-established processes of mediation and arbitration to Internet based services like Cybersettle that may facilitate the resolution of disputes in less time and at a lower cost without resort to the public court system. Lawyers have a role to play in these alternatives. They have for many years been assisting clients in mediations and arbitrations. Some lawyers focus on these types of dispute resolution and assist their clients in developing their presentations and presenting their arguments to best advantage.

Founded in 1998, Cybersettle states that it is the world's largest online claims settlement service. It utilizes a patented double-blind bid auction system that has processed hundreds of thousands of transactions and facilitated more than $1.8 billion in transactional value of insurance claims while often reducing the claims cycle by four to six months. Its system is also frequently used in healthcare and public disputes. The largest settlement said to have been achieved using its service has been $12.5 million.

E-Bay provides a similar service to resolve disputes relating to the sale and purchase of goods on E-Bay. There will be more such electronic systems that may have an adverse effect on business of lawyers serving the relatively high frequency-small claims part of the legal market.

I doubt that the desired improvements in cost-effectiveness of our legal system can be achieved by technological and operational improvements alone. Some of my thoughts on reforming our multi-layered legal system can be found in chapter 10 of *Profit and the Practice of Law*, "Reforming the Legal System."

CHAPTER ELEVEN

Legal Education

L egal education traditionally involves the study of a wide range of legal subjects that usually includes required courses in civil procedure, contracts, criminal law, legislation and regulation, torts, and real estate, and elective courses in an array of legal subjects such as accounting, administrative procedure, anti-trust and trade regulation, agency, business planning, commercial transactions, constitutional issues, corporations, employment, environmental regulation, estates and trusts, finance and securities, international law and transactions, labor, litigation, mergers and acquisitions, partnership, taxation, etc.

Today many practicing lawyers work in only one or two of these fields of specialization despite the fact that they have all received instruction in law school in many of them. Most large firm associates are recruited to work in specific firm departments, and they are seldom asked to address issues outside of their area of specialization.

Until the latter part of the 20th Century most of the training young lawyers received in the practice of law was provided by the more senior attorneys in their first law firm. As law firm leverage increased and revenues generated became more important in determining lawyer compensation, the amount of time senior lawyers chose to commit to training law school graduates decreased; consequently, many of today's young lawyers have not received the training required to effectively provide the legal services that clients require. In addition, as the law and law firm operations have grown increasingly complex it is taking more time and experience for young lawyers to learn their trade and to develop the know-how and relationships necessary to represent clients effectively.

There are increasing efforts to transfer the responsibility for the vocational training of new lawyers to the law schools, but the schools generally are not structured or staffed to assume that responsibility. Most law school faculty members have practiced law for a relatively short period of time before entering the teaching profession. As a result, many of them have not learned how to practice law in the real world and do not have the experience that they are being asked to impart to their students. Consequently, many law schools are using experienced practicing lawyers as adjunct professors in an effort to provide some of the desired training.

Law school clinical programs may provide some useful knowledge and experience to those students interested in litigation and dispute resolution, but are generally inadequate for those students interested in pursuing corporate and business law. The clinical programs usually focus on the unserved or underserved portions of the market for legal services and have little relevance to the services provided by larger business oriented law firms.

In addition, most law schools have largely ignored the growing employment prospects for legal professionals who would like to be prepared to hold administrative and support jobs rather than becoming traditional practicing lawyers; they have not altered their curricula to prepare their graduates for such jobs. They also are not participating in the education and training of legal assistants who are being hired in increasing numbers by law firms and law departments.

Much has been written of late about the costs and burdens of our existing three year law degree regimes and I do not propose to weigh into that fight which is being addressed by others. However there are a couple of observations I would like to make about legal education in general. Back in the 1950s and 1960s most lawyers when necessary were expected to learn on their own without the benefit of classroom instruction areas of the law that they had not studied in law school. I doubt that three years of study of various legal subjects is necessary to satisfactorily develop this skill. None of us can anticipate all of the legal knowledge we will need in our practices and study it in law school. In addition, much of the required knowledge will change over a long legal career.

As a result, all new lawyers are likely to have to learn a good deal of law on their own. Consequently, in lieu of one of the usual highly structured legal subject matter courses, law schools could offer a course that would help prepare young lawyers to conduct their own future legal education. In addition, if legal-hybrid practitioners are going to be in demand, then joint degree programs should be coordinated with other university schools and departments.

Most law schools do not offer courses in the evolution of the practice of law in modern times, law practice economics, or law practice management. I believe that law schools should offer courses on law practice management and economics, as well as a course that focuses on preparing law graduates for work in the in-house law departments of businesses, not-for-profit organizations, and government agencies.

A small number of law departments are now employing law graduates directly out of law school rather than relying on private practice firms to train them first. There are good reasons for doing so because some of the habits young lawyers acquire in private practice may be counterproductive in the law department environment, and increased leverage and focus on profits have reduced the willingness and ability of many law firms to provide basic training.

Reducing the cost of a law school education is an admirable and appropriate goal. If my recollection is correct, the tuition at Harvard Law School in the 1961-62 school year was $1,250. Adjusted for inflation that tuition would be about $10,000 today. In fact, today's tuition at Harvard Law for one year is $59,555 (almost six times the inflation adjusted amount). Many of the leading law schools charge similar amounts. Of course, we got a splendid legal education in the early 1960s, so it is not clear how the current curriculum and programs provide students with more than five times the value law school students received over 50 years ago.

The high cost of obtaining a legal education today is one of the greatest obstacles to the provision of adequate legal services to the unserved and underserved portions of our population. Lawyers who have borrowed substantial sums to pay for their college and legal educations probably cannot service their loans and maintain a comfortable standard of living for themselves and their families unless they charge for their services fees that the unserved and underserved markets cannot afford.

Unlike many medical schools that have affiliated nursing schools, law schools generally have not undertaken to participate in the education of secondary level legal professional personnel that work in law departments and law firms, or paralawyers who may work on their own. I believe law schools would benefit from providing some of the necessary training for paralegals and paralawyers which might improve the integration of paralegal and paralawyer support personnel into the legal services process as well as using some of the law school facilities and professionals that may otherwise be redundant. While some schools offer joint JD-MBA programs, they tend to operate independently.

The system of legal education in the United States has contributed to the decline of legal craftsmanship and the loss of understanding of how the common law legal system is supposed to work. The law is taught in law schools by the use of "casebooks," which present "the law" by quoting from cases drawn from various U.S. jurisdictions, and occasionally foreign ones, selected by the authors because of the skill of a particular judge in illuminating the issues, or because the author thought the conclusion reached was correct, or at least worthy of consideration. In class, students are called upon to "state the case;" to tell the facts of the case in their text book, what the court decided, and to analyze the court's reasoning. In this process, a case from one jurisdiction is as good as one from another. Every case is "binding precedent" in the classroom.

Graduates of our law schools practice law much the way they learn it, as do the lawyers who become judges. Law schools generally do not place enough emphasis on the role of *stare decisis* ("it is decided") and of binding precedent on the judicial process in a particular jurisdiction. They look far and wide for a case that supports the position they advocate without regard to its relevance within their own jurisdiction; the resulting loss to the profession of legal craftsmanship—the precise and disciplined use of relevant judicial precedent—has been a regrettable lapse in legal education.

American law schools need to consider the risk to which they are exposed by the growth in opportunities for legal service providers who are not licensed lawyers. Because law departments (or for that matter, law firms) can employ the services of a useful professional who is not a member of the bar to advise them with respect to a particular issue (such as acquiring other businesses), the opportunity exists for individuals to obtain an education for such roles without taking the time and incurring the expense involved in learning about a lot of other legal issues that are not relevant to their desired expertise.

M&A lawyers may find themselves competing with an "acquisition specialist" with a business degree in "mergers and acquisitions" who has taken a year or more of legal course work focusing on the subject. While such a person would not be in a position to give a "legal opinion" on the ultimate agreement, such opinions are less likely to be required these days, and the client's in-house staff could provide whatever pure legal advice might be necessary.

For those readers interested in the many current issues in legal education, I recommend Professor Brian Tamanaha's excellent book on the subject: *Failing Law Schools* (Univ. of Chicago Press, 2012).

CHAPTER TWELVE

Looking Forward

Many hundreds of years ago, in the early days of lawyering, lawyers were the primary source of information about the law, as well as the interpretation and application of the law, because most folks couldn't read, and in any event, hand copied texts were few and far between. The printing press made it possible to put the law in books for use by people who could read and afford to own them, and over the centuries books became commonplace and relatively inexpensive.

The move from print-based legal information to Internet based legal information has made it easier for many people to gain direct access to legal information in many of its forms; but increasing the availability of legal information has not significantly increased the percentage of the population capable of coping with the law without professional assistance.

Legal information is the starting point of legal analysis, but it is only a part of the process of identifying relevant facts and law, reaching factual and legal conclusions, formulating legal strategy, and taking legal action. In order to achieve a successful resolution of most legal issues much more than information is required. Computers can help find legal information that in simple cases may suffice for legal action, but for many situations legal information by itself cannot lead to a successful legal result.

If access to legal information were all that was required to understand and function effectively within the legal system, the legal profession would have shrunk years ago. For the various reasons set forth in Chapter Six, there is a good deal more to the use and management of the legal system than the ability to find and read statutes, regulations, cases and commentary.

We also know that the practice of law and the delivery of legal services have changed significantly since the end of World War II, and we know how lawyers, law firms and law departments have contributed to such changes and adjusted to them. We have also explored the key developments during the last 70+ years that have made such changes possible, necessary and even desirable for many lawyers and firms. There is a tendency for some consultants and academics to call these changes "disruptive innovations" when for the most part they are simply interesting and challenging changes that have improved the quality of legal service delivery.

We have also explored changes likely to occur in the foreseeable future in the ways that legal services are provided to the organizations and individuals needing them and changes in the way disputes are resolved in our legal system, as well as the effect of such changes on the economics of the practice of law.

Aside from successful plaintiffs' lawyers, a high percentage of the money available to lawyers for their services comes from clients with significant financial resources. As a result, many more lawyers are drawn to the major business legal practice than there is such work for them to do.

The recent excess supply of law school graduates seeking to serve these portions of the legal services market has not yet significantly reduced the cost of such services, in part because of the growing size and complexity of the national and world economies, and in part because of the long time span required for new lawyers to absorb and apply the knowledge and to develop the know-how needed to address more complex and challenging legal issues. It is likely that downward pressure on legal fees will increase as the excess supply of law graduates is absorbed into the work force and as they are fully integrated into the profession.

It is also likely to be somewhat more difficult for lawyers to establish and operate profitable solo practices or small firms because of the high cost of the hardware, software and training necessary to establish a modern law practice, and their need to amortize the increasingly high cost of their legal educations. Alternative legal service providers, and in some states licensed paralawyers, are now providing some of the services that previously helped to support many sole practitioners and small firms, and provided the training of young lawyers in small and medium-sized law practices.

ALSPs have found effective ways to compete with law firms in the provision of some legal and related services both by reorganizing the ways such services are staffed and provided, and by supplying those services directly to clients and law departments at lower prices. Such lower prices are possible in part because of their effective utilization of technology and less expensive personnel. Improving technology and software programs will aid the movement in-house of more legal work by providing law departments with greater, faster and more user-friendly access to legal knowledge and know-how at less cost.

Most medium-sized organizations have at least one in-house lawyer/legal executive to manage their legal work, and many small organizations do as well. These organizations will continue to use outside lawyers to provide many required services when they lack anyone in-house with the necessary expertise, or to deal with periodic overloads arising from acquisitions, financings and disputes, among other things. The lawyers and firms servicing such clients will, of course, also face pressure to provide more cost-effective legal services.

Organizations with large law departments will from time to time be in need for law firms and law specialists to assist them with sporadic overloads or important or esoteric issues beyond their expertise levels.

I do not foresee the disappearance of small and medium-sized law firms serving the middle and upper end of the individual market for legal services or the small and medium-sized organization market. And some solo practitioners and small firms may find a way through the use of technology and trained but lower cost nonlawyer personnel to profitably serve parts of the underserved and unserved markets. Some of these practices may be housed more conveniently to the public in shopping malls, banks or retail establishments. And some of these practices are likely to become less profitable, just as the practices of many of the major business practice firms are likely to become less profitable for many of their lawyers, because of technology, better management (inside and outside) and competition from a plentiful supply of capable lawyers, law firms, law departments, paralawyers, and ALSPs.

The migration of compensation levels downward closer to the historical norm will not decimate the legal profession, but the combination of large college and law school loans and lower compensation are likely to lower the standard of living of many of the next generation of practicing lawyers. Many will not have the very high level of prosperity that their predecessors have enjoyed in recent years and that they may have anticipated when they enrolled in law school. But lower profitability will not lead to extinction, and smaller law school enrollments will in due course bring the supply of lawyers into better balance.

It is nonetheless likely over the near term that many law graduates will have to find other ways to sustain themselves and their families—there are just too many of them now to be absorbed into the profession—and many may find better opportunities in other fields. Some will be successful traditional general practitioners in smaller or rural communities where there is a shortage of lawyers, and some will be able to develop enough expertise in a particular subject or locale to sustain their practice. Others may become successful business entrepreneurs founding legal technology start-ups with venture capital funding.

The limited number of Elite Firms will be providing legal services very profitably far into the future, and their profitability will hold up better than the profits of the next tier of major firms including the major international firms (unless they are also truly expert firms) because, by definition, the most expert firms, despite their high prices, will be in demand to work on the most important deals and "bet-the-company" situations.

Many law firms continue to be faced with the necessity of figuring out what services their current and potential clients need and what the clients are willing to pay for those services, and then they must refashion their practice to respond to those needs. What is their market or markets? How will these markets best be served? And what needs to be done in order to supply the services required at a price prospective clients are able and willing to pay?

Most of the people who have become lawyers are very self-confident. Few of us would have gotten to where we are today if we were not. Our surplus of self-confidence will only complicate and intensify the competition among lawyers and law firms for the legal business still available to them. Most of us think we are smart enough and can work hard enough to outperform our competition. Consequently, the battle for survival and profitability is likely to be arduous and continuing.

EPILOGUE

There is one major issue that requires additional comment and discussion before concluding my analysis of the prospects for the legal profession. That issue is the extent to which automation (including "Artificial Intelligence") may reduce the need for lawyers in the future.

As noted in Chapter Two, there has been a huge growth in the size and complexity of the economies of the United States and of the world since the end of World War II that has contributed to a tremendous growth in local, state, national and international laws and regulations. During this time technology in the form of dictation machines, copiers, printers, computers, software programs, cell phones, the Internet and e-mail has significantly affected how law is practiced in the United States without reducing the need for a growing number of lawyers. As in the past, the number of lawyers required to provide legal services in the future will be positively affected by continued population, economic and governmental growth, and negatively affected by efficiencies resulting from technological advances.

A significant part of the profession's growth in recent decades has been the result of the need for more lawyers (and paralegals) to conduct "due diligence" review and analysis of the increasingly numerous, lengthy and complex documents resulting from increasingly large and complex transactions and disputes. However, recently developed document review and predictive coding technologies have reduced the need for many of the associates and paralegals who provided these services in the past.

The question remains whether automation technology in the future will significantly reduce the need for human lawyers. I don't think so, and many knowledgeable legal technology experts don't think so either.

There are four major factors that will continue to support the need for more lawyers. The first two were noted at the beginning of Chapter Two: increased national and international economic and political activity, in part attributable to population growth, and the growing bodies of laws and regulations at every level of government (local, state, national and international) created to manage such increased activity.

The third factor is the large current unmet need for legal services. To the extent that automation will enable lawyers to provide legal services more cost-effectively, the financially profitable market for legal services is likely to expand to include more of the currently underserved and unserved markets.

The fourth factor supporting the continued need for a large and robust legal profession is the inadequacy of present and anticipated advances in automation to manage adequately many aspects of legal service.

I believe that the continuing growth of population, economies, and governmental regulation, as in the past, will likely provide more jobs for lawyers than will be lost to the increasing use of automation to support or provide legal services.

In reaching these conclusions I have relied on a number of studies by experts on automation, as well as on my own understanding of the skills lawyers utilize in serving the needs of their clients. One of best of these studies entitled *Can Robots Be Lawyers? Computers, Lawyers, and the Practice of Law* was produced by Dana Remus, a Professor of Law at the University of North Carolina's School of Law, and Frank Levy, a Professor Emeritus at MIT. Another important study is in a series of articles on the prospects for automation produced by the McKinsey Global Institute. I recommend that any prospective law student or practicing lawyer interested in the possible effects of automation on the practice of law consult these studies in their entirety.

Remus and Levy, after a thoughtful analysis of how lawyers function, concluded "that automation has an impact on the demand for lawyer's time that while measureable, is far less significant than popular accounts suggest." They recommend "that the existing literature's narrow focus on employment effects should be broadened to include the many ways in which computers are changing (as opposed to replacing) the work of lawyers."

They conclude that "computer technology is the most advanced in the areas of document review and document management" and "is the least advanced in the areas of legal writing, advising clients, communications and interactions, factual investigation, negotiations, and court appearances." I note that these "least advanced areas" are among those that cause the practice of law to be much more than an information service.

Remus and Levy estimate that approximately 13% of the work lawyers currently do could be performed by existing computer technology and they assume that it would likely take five years or more to acquire the equipment and to train the personnel necessary to accomplish this replacement—if and when law firms and law departments make the decision to do so.

Digital McKinsey has produced a series of several articles since November of 2015 on the subject of "digital disruption" and has focused on digital reinvention in many occupations including the practice of law. The McKinsey study has estimated that approximately 23% of the work currently done by lawyers and 69% of the legal work currently performed by paralegals could be automated by adapting currently demonstrated technology.

In a July 2016 McKinsey article entitled *Where machines could replace humans—and where they can't (yet)* McKinsey identified five qualities that are the necessary precondition for automation. The first is technical feasibility, the second is the cost of developing and deploying the necessary hardware and software, the third is the cost of labor compared to the cost of alternatives, the fourth is the benefits beyond labor substitution—"higher output, better quality and fewer errors," and the fifth is regulatory and social-acceptance issues. "The potential for automation to take hold in a sector or occupation reflects a subtle interplay between these factors and the trade-offs among them."

The McKinsey article also noted that: "Even when machines do take over some human activities in an occupation, this does not necessarily spell the end of the jobs in that line of work. On the contrary, their number at times increases in occupations that have been partly automated, because overall demand for their remaining activities has continued to grow."

The article goes on to say that: "The hardest activities to automate with currently available technologies are those that involve managing and developing people (9 percent automation potential) or that apply expertise to decision making, planning, or creative work (18 percent). These activities, often characterized as knowledge work, can be as varied as coding software, creating menus, or writing promotional materials. For now, computers do an excellent job with very well-defined activities . . . but humans still need to determine the proper goals, interpret results, or provide commonsense checks for solutions."

"As stated at the offset, though, simply considering the technical potential for automation is not enough to assess how much of it will occur in particular activities. The actual level will reflect the interplay of the technical potential, the benefits and costs (or the business case), the supply-and-demand dynamics of labor, and various regulatory and social factors related to acceptability."

There is another important issue affecting the need for new law school graduates; the remarkable decline in the number of law students at a time when the number of lawyers reaching retirement age is increasing significantly. First year law school enrollment in the 2016-2017 school year was 37,107 versus the average first year enrollment over the last 43 years of 43,471. If this trend continues there will be many more lawyers retiring in the years ahead than there will be recent graduates to take their place. Rather than displacing lawyers, increased technological progress may be necessary to enable a shrinking number of lawyers to provide the legal services required.

Based on the referenced studies and on my own experience and analysis, I think the world will continue to require more legal services and more lawyers to provide them. Lawyers, as they have in the past, will continue to use technological advances to provide more efficiently a growing volume of legal work, but the increasing growth in population and in the economies of the world will create more governmental regulation and a need for more lawyers to provide such services. Because I do not expect human nature to undergo a comprehensive transformation, I am optimistic about the future of the legal profession.

THE END

CPSIA information can be obtained
at www.ICGtesting.com
Printed in the USA
LVHW110821180722
723712LV00005B/362